THE ACTOR'S HUSTLE

A STEP BY STEP GUIDE TO GETTING YOUR FOOT IN THE DOOR IN TV AND FILM AND HOW TO MAKE MONEY WITH YOUR CRAFT

BY SHANA SOLOMON
WITH CARLINGTON NEIL

All rights reserved under the international and Pan-American copyright conventions. First published in the United States of America. All rights reserved. With the exception of brief quotations in a review, no part of this book may be reproduced or transmitted, in any form, or by any means, electronic or mechanical (including photocopying), nor may it be stored in any information storage and retrieval system without written permission from the publisher.

DISCLAIMER

The advice contained in this material might not be suitable for everyone. The author designed the information to present her opinion about the subject matter. The reader must carefully investigate all aspects of any business decision before committing him or herself. The author obtained the information contained herein form sources she believes to be reliable and from her own personal experience, but she neither implies nor intends any guarantee of accuracy. The author is not in the business of giving legal, accounting, or any other type of professional advice. Should the reader need such advice, he or she must seek services from a competent professional. The author particularly disclaims any liability, loss, or risk taken by individuals who directly or indirectly act on the information contained herein. The author believes the advice presented here is sound, but readers cannot hold her responsible for either the actions they take or the risk taken by individuals who directly or indirectly act on the information contained herein.

Published by 1BrickPublishing
Printed in the United States
Cover Design by @PixelStudio
Copyright © 2019 by Shana Solomon
ISBN 978-1-949303-07-0

This book is dedicated to the millions of actors who need help in moving forward in their careers. Today is the beginning of your brand-new life. Get ready.

Contents

Acknowledgements 7

About The Author 9

Introduction 12

The Leap 20

The Hustle 46

The Struggle 118

Stay In It 124

Own Your Image 142

Your Mental Health 146

You Did That!!!!!! 168

The Actors Hustle QnA Workbook. 172

Acknowledgements

To my beautiful angel, my mother, Karen A. Solomon. This book would've never happened without you for many reasons including your support, long talks, annoying but beautiful lessons and your belief in me. You were my cheerleader squad on earth but I know you're still cheering for me from above. I love you. To my love, Carlington, you are amazing for literally helping me write this book out in Starbucks and kept the lattes coming for energy along with words of perfection that I could never dream of coming up with. You are a smooth ass wordsmith and I am grateful for your consistent encouragement to write and put this book out into the world and become a better version of myself. I love and appreciate your heart and your hustle. You are magical. To my dad, all of my many amazing teachers, coaches, family and friends, thank you for helping me, supporting me, pushing me and keeping it real with me. You are a huge reason why this book exists and I love you all.

About The Author

Shana Solomon is from the Bronx, New York and has studied acting for almost 20 years. She is an author, writer, producer and an award-winning character actor known for her recurring role as Karen on NBC's Shades Of Blue" starring Jennifer Lopez and Ray Liotta. As well as her other roles on "POWER", NBC's "New Amsterdam", "Law & Order SVU", BET's "First Wives Club", "Modern Love" Steven Spielberg's and Ed Burns' "Public Morals", HBO's "Divorce", "The Deuce" and TNT's "Search Party" to name a few.

Solomon was also featured in the Oscar nominated film, 'The Big Sick' as well 'as crown heights', 'The Set UP', starring Lucy Liu and Taye Diggs and 'First One In'. She also co-wrote, produced and starred in an award-winning short film, "Cool Kidz", about inner city bullying in the Bronx. Shana has starred in countless films and National commercials.

Shana's most talked about project is her one-woman show, "THE CLOSET B.I.T.C.H", a dark comedy about a woman who tries not to fall apart while she does everything in her power to make everyone else happy. Shana created, produced, wrote, and plays 19 different characters in the live show. The Closet B.I.T.C.H just recently had a 54 show run with 46 sold out shows off-off Broadway in New York City and is now gearing up for her next run and tour of her hit one woman show, please visit TheClosetBitch.com for tickets and news.

Solomon also co-produced, co-created and co-wrote "The Closet B.I.T.C.H" web-series with theater and film director William Alexander Runnels. The series can be currently found on YouTube.

THE ACTORS HUSTLE

A step-by-step guide on how to get your foot in the door in TV & Film and start making money with your craft.

"I want to act. I want to play characters that are multi dimensional and that showcase my gifts and talents that are attached to a great story. But I also want to be able to pay my damn bills and afford the lifestyle that I desire."
~
Shana A. Solomon

Introduction

I want this book to be your guide to getting your shit together as an actor. I want it to help you begin your journey by getting your foot in the door and becoming a successful working actor. Many new actors always ask me, "How did you do it?

Where do I start?" I say, "it's simple, you just dive right in and here's how…. " I just wish someone would've given me a book just like this when I first started out 14 years ago. But then, I wouldn't have written this bad boy your currently reading.

Just to be super clear, I am not an acting teacher or an acting coach. I am a working actor that has experienced 14 years of grinding, hustling, failing and winning that put a guide together based off what worked for me and other successful actors I know so you don't take as long as I did and fail as much as I did to accomplish your acting goals and dreams.

This is my story guys…

Introduction

It's real, raw, uncut and relates to just about every actor who has a day or night job to support their passion for acting or still trying to figure it all out. I've been where you are, so let me connect with you first by telling you my story and then we will get to the GOLD on how you can leave that Day job and start making money from acting in TV & in Film.

Why did I write this book?

Ever since I starred in "Cin-Day" the ghetto version of Cinderella, in my 4th grade class' theater performance, I knew acting was not only my gift but it was exactly what I wanted to do. The feeling that came over me as soon as I stepped on that stage felt like I was home. It instantly became my happy place. The reaction I got on that stage from the actors who I either threw off or helped shine sparked something unexplainable yet perfect inside me. Even at that age I knew how to live in the moment and under imaginary circumstances. I loved how the audience reacted to our performance. There's nothing like that live reaction from a theater full of people who are laughing and on the edge of their seats and taking that ride with you as the story unfolds where you could either hear a pin drop or hear every gasp. But once the show was over, it was difficult to hold onto that feeling in my everyday life. Everyone around me including my closest friends all wanted to be nurses, doctors or even just make enough money to live a good life. None of them, I repeat, none of them had the aspirations to do what most of society considers impossible, "Become a famous and successful actor". If they did, they never expressed it like me. I mean, I would tell everyone that came in my presence that I wanted to be the next Julia Roberts, Meryl Streep or female Denzel or De Niro. Everyone who knew me knew my personality was perfect for it. I'm super creative and I watch movies the way ball players practice to win. I can watch movies alllll damn day! I'm in love with great writing, amazing acting, a perfect story and beautiful cinematography. I have been studying actors on screen since I was a child because my father would put me in front of the TV and hand me the remote while he did whatever he needed to do. The actors on TV and in Film practically raised me and helped my imagination grow. And the older I got, the more I started to relate to them and what they were going through. It became a part of my life in a sense. It's something that just clicked with me and spoke to my soul and I honestly couldn't ignore it. I knew I would become an actor because it never felt out of reach to me. Even though I was living in Co-Op City in the North East Bronx as well as Prospect Ave and Jackson Projects in the South Bronx, which is surrounded by poverty and pain, I knew I would rise above all of that and become one of those actors I'd seen on TV and in the movies if I just went for it.

So lets fast forward to the part where I have about $2200 in bills per month, dropped out of college because it wasn't drama focused even though it was a "performing arts school", they didn't allow any drama majors to audition or act until their junior year. which I thought was complete bullshit. Everyone around me is telling me I need a "plan B" to make money in order to support my "Play A" which is acting. So I'm now fake smiling and greeting every single customer that walks into this high-end handbag store in the Westchester Mall in White Plains, New York. I constantly fix and sell monogrammed and leather handbags that topple onto the floor in order to pay my bills. I'm not in any kind of acting class or school, I'm not auditioning, I don't hang around any actors, nor do I have a plan as to how I'm going to become an actor in place. All I'm doing is working that "plan B" unclear, unmotivated and slowly dying inside because I know I'm better than this. But then something magical happens.

As I'm fake smiling and greeting a rowdy family of 8 that walks into the store and thinking to myself, "how am I going to get out of here and become the actress I was meant to be?" I looked up, past the set of tantrum crying twins in some name brand ridiculously expensive stroller and I saw Spike Lee walking with his wife right outside my store! I started to just walk right out of the store to talk to Spike but then I realized I was the only person on the sales floor.

But I didn't want to miss my opportunity to talk to Spike. I wanted to ask him a few questions on what I can do to get my foot in the door or if I could intern for him. Just as I had that thought I saw them walk up to Starbucks so I knew I had a little time. I ran to call my manager who was downstairs doing inventory, "Hey Drew! Can you please come upstairs really quickly, I want to take a quick 5 minute break. Spike Lee's outside and I wanna meet him!" DREW: "Ugggghhhhh, I'm doing inventory right now and it's just us". ME: "Yeah I know, but this is super important, it'll only take 5 minutes, not even! Please Drew! Your know acting is like my world and Spike Lee is outside at Starbucks!" DREW: "But inventory has to get done ASAP and so honestly. Iiiiiii can't" ME: "Drew I only need like 2 minutes, Please I'll stay late and help you get inventory done whatever it takes I'll be right back!" DREW: "Shana I can't, I'm sorry." Drew hung up the phone. Now the younger me who lived in the south Bronx would've just walked out of that store and said "Fuck this Job" and spoke to Spike Lee. But this new me with new bills and no plan for my plan A just stood there feeling helpless, weak, and totally out of control of my life. I watched as Spike lee and his wife ordered coffee and Slowly, not even briskly but sloowwly walked away into the mall abyss.

So I had time to sneak out and come back without my manager knowing I was even gone. But I was too in my head in that moment. I didn't even race around the mall looking for him. I'd already decided speaking to Spike wouldn't happen. I had envisioned my failure and accepted my defeat. That night when my manager finished inventory and came upstairs, he looked like he felt he had accomplished something great. He looked relieved and refreshed and actually happy that he did what he set out to do that day. While I felt hopeless, pissed off and enraged. I wanted to blame my manager for not letting me speak to Spike Lee but I realized in that moment it wasn't my managers fault at all and it wasn't even necessarily about speaking to Spike because If I had a plan in place where I was properly using my "Plan B" to finance and support my "Plan A" then I wouldn't put my dreams of becoming an actor into the hands of even one of my idols like, Spike Lee. Because what if Spike said, "I really don't feel like being bothered with anybody today kid"? Would I feel the same or even worse? I realized because of what happened, I was putting the power and the control of my personal destiny into the hands of others and wasn't taking any control of my dreams. I had no goals and no idea as to how I was going to become a successful actor. So what, was I expecting Spike Lee to give me a step by step conversation as to how to become one? Yes. Would he have probably done it? I doubt it. Maybe he would've said some encouraging words like, "Don't ever quit", and that would've definitely felt great and given me some momentary inspiration but then what? Was I going to put "Don't quit" into action steps as to how to become a working actor? Probably not, because I met Angelina Jolie A few years prior to that in a retail shop called Patricia Fields down in SoHo in NYC and she said the most amazing thing to me, Angelina Jolie said, "You are absolutely beautiful, if you want to act, you will act, just do it, it's going to happen." And what did I do with her words? I went and got a damn retail job (insert eye-roll emoji). So, I wanted to tell you this story to show you that the power that it takes to get on TV and in Films, if you want to keep your dignity, is already inside of YOU. It takes YOU to decide when you are going after your own dreams and it takes YOU to hustle and be motivated enough to push and take the necessary steps everyday towards achieving your goals. All you need is a plan and the passion and persistence to make it. And my goal is to give you what you need in order to create your plan and inspire you to HUSTLE that plan until you reach your goal. I'm talking about a plan on how to use your day job or "Plan B" to make sure your "Plan A" which is your goal of getting your foot in the door and start making money acting in TV & Film. I have developed a few different step by step action plans and ideas, depending on your style of hustle, that has not only worked for me but has worked for many other actors who went from never being on TV or in a studio film to getting their foot in the door, acting on TV, in studio films, and even reaching their goals of becoming a series regular, a household name and more! But you have to follow either the action steps I suggest in this book or another industry professionals' steps who has done it themselves or shown others how and have positive results from their teachings. Now I have to be honest. The action steps that I have put together for you in this book aren't the only ways an actor should hustle to reach their goals of getting their foot in the door. I'm sure there are many other ways. It's super important you create and or follow an action plan that works for YOU. I'm giving you plans that worked for ME and got me co-starring, guest starring roles, a recurring role on TV and in an Oscar nominated film. It also worked for other actors that hustled these same action steps in this book to reach their goals of being on TV and in studio films. My actor friends used to call me up all the time and ask me how I got my foot in the door and what did I do to get on Power, Law & Order or in A Super Bowl Commercial or in an Oscar nominated film? I would give them the exact same gems and secrets that I'm giving YOU in this book. So after witnessing and experiencing the results from my step by step informative and motivational phone calls and giving actors a way to hustle in this industry and get their foot in the door, I decided to write a book to reach as many actors as I could because I wish I would've read something just like this when I first started out 14 years ago.

*"Do not allow the work and the struggle to deter you, nothing worth having comes easy." –***Shana A. Solomon**

"What ever your dream is, every extra penny needs to be going to that." – **Will Smith**

"Be happy you have a Bartending, serving, dog walking, barista, 9-5 or night job. Because you're going to take every penny that doesn't go to your bills and creature needs and put it towards your dreams and goals of becoming the best actor." -**Shana Solomon**

*"Bet every dollar on yourself. You have more control over the outcome." -**Shana Solomon***

My goal is to guide you on how to hustle in this acting industry to reach your goal

Having Unstoppable Systems To Leverage Everything

1

The Leap

Okay, so, let's just say you're currently at ground zero. Ground zero is you either haven't taken any action yet towards your goal of becoming an actor or you haven't booked a speaking role or the type of roles you're interested in and have been shooting for like guest starring or a series regular role on a network TV, a major streaming platform such a NETFLIX or in a Studio film and you're either being supported by an awesome human being who believes in your dreams and goals of becoming a successful A-List actor Or you have a day job until you become a successful A-List actor. If you haven't taken any action yet towards your goal of becoming a successful actor this book is perfect for you and if you have taken action like taken acting classes, booked a few roles and even have representation but you're not being sent out the way you want to be and would like to take your career to the next level by booking a co-starring, guest-starring, guest-recurring, recurring or series regular role on TV or a major supporting or lead role in a studio film, this book is also perfect for you. Regardless of where you are in your career, let's say you're at a brand-new starting point on your journey to become a successful working actor and soon to be household name.

So what do you do from right where you are?

*It's super important to create a whole new environment for yourself that supports your acting goals as much as possible.

My first and most important habit to live by as an actor is to surround myself with other actors. And even more importantly, surround myself with actors who are either at a similar place in their career as I am or further along in their careers than I am so I can follow in their footsteps and be motivated to do so. There's nothing better than your acting buddy calling you up in full excitement and telling you that they just booked the lead role in a hit new MARVEL COMIC film and tells you the scoop on exactly how they went about doing it. You are supposed to be excited with all your soul for them, listen, soak up all that amazing energy and learn. That phone call is supposed to feed you and give you great energy, good vibes and hope knowing that your day of doing something super similar is on it's way.

*There is no room for jealousy in this industry. There are enough roles for all of us. I have gone on auditions where the entire room of 12 women looked just like me in terms of weight, height, skin complexion and even though only one of us books that job, I have seen all of us on TV or on the movie screen at some point. If you stay in it and stay genuinely happy for others and know that each of us books acting jobs that are designed specifically for us you will be much happier in this business. Remember, what is for you is for you.

So how can you surround yourself with other actors as well as actors who are where you want to be?

1) GET IN A GREAT ACTING CLASS

Now when I say an acting class I don't necessarily mean go sign up and pay for some Ivy League performing arts school or even a 4-year drama program. Even though, those are extremely great ways of surrounding yourself with other actors, I'm just saying that is not your only option and unless you get a scholarship, grant, financial aid or have the ability to pay for those schools as well as the time, they can be super expensive and put you in a world of debt. There are tons of shorter and less expensive ongoing acting schools, studios and classes that you can jump into at different times throughout the year that works with many different types of schedules. Most upcoming actors have full time day or night or attend other schools, classes and or have children. Nowadays there is no excuse why you can't take an acting class. There is a perfect fit for you; you just have to find it. And I can help you with that. But acting classes not only help you surround yourself with other actors including working actors but also, help you to awaken your acting spirit! Taking an acting class is also a surefire way to get more in touch and familiar with yourself and learn more about whom you really are. Almost all actors become more self-aware and gain a better understanding of themselves, their motivation, goals and desires. And on top of all that, you will get some amazing training while you're there. I went to **The Deena Levy Theater Studio in NYC**. It was a weekly 4-hour class. I decided to take a theater class because I wanted to acquire the raw; in your face acting skills that theater requires and have that classic New York Theater training foundation under my belt. I learned The *Meisner Technique* in Deena's class. The Meisner Technique teaches you to "live truthfully under imaginary circumstances". There are many other techniques out there but I decided to start with this method fist since I felt like I already knew how to do that and it resonated with my spirit. As soon as I took that leap of faith and jumped into Deena's class, I quickly realized I didn't know how to live truthfully under imaginary circumstances as well as I thought I did with also memorizing a script and applying the skill to someone else's words and world. So you might think, "I don't need to get into a class or a school. I know what I'm doing." And you might be right, but you never know what you else you may learn about that particular technique or even about yourself that will be super important to your growth as an actor. Also, you get to meet some amazing actors who might end up being your support group and circle of positivity in this industry when times get rough. I still speak to a few of my actor friends who are now starring in shows like "The House of Flowers" on Netflix and "Black Lighting" on the CW. These are actors who I've had countless motivational convo's with over the years before we all "Made it" and helped each other keep our heads in the game and continued to Hustle.

There are Soooooooo many acting schools, studios and classes to take in NYC, LA, and ATL & NEW ORLEANS. Like The Deena Levy Theater Studio or Esper studios in NYC or Howard Fine Acting Studio and The Ivana Chubbuck Studio in LA. You can also find a list of more my favorite schools as well as a few top-rated schools in those areas by visiting theactorshustle.com for resources. Please remember to do your own research before making a commitment to any of my suggested resources. Make sure they are right for you.

> *"Study, find all the good teachers and study with them, get involved in acting to act, not to be famous or for the money. Do plays. It's not worth it if you are just in it for the money. You have to love it."* **–Phillip Seymour Hoffman**

> *"Acting is behaving truthfully under imaginary circumstances."* **–Sanford Meisner**

Whether you choose to get a BA or MFA in performing arts, attend a conservatory or a take acting classes at a program, studio or workshop, you should know the different acting techniques that are out there and decide which one speaks to you because you will be spending anywhere from 8-60 hours per week learning it, breathing it and becoming it.

7 Acting Techniques

1) Stanislavski's System – Constantin Stanislavski's approach incorporates spiritual realism, emotional memory, dramatic and self-analysis, and disciplined practice.

2) Lee Strasberg's "THE METHOD" – Came from the Stanislavski approach. The Method encourages actors to magnify their connection to the material by creating their characters' emotional experiences in their own lives. Angelina Jolie, Jared Leto, Jake Gyllenhaal, Scarlett Johansson, Steve Buscemi, Al Pacino, Alec Baldwin, Dustin Hoffman, Paul Newman, Marilyn Monroe. James Dean & Ellen Burstyn were trained with the Strasberg "Method" technique.

3) Meisner Technique - Sanford Meisner developed his technique in the 1930's. He taught acting for over 65 years. Meisner created a technique that would turn actors into spontaneous, impulsive, instinctive, present, human, free, fearless, authentic, moment-to-moment machines. (Taken from the Meisner technique studio website) It's a process that helps you get out of your head and into your gut. He teaches you to live truthfully under imaginary circumstances. He has a famous exercise called "repetition", where 2 actors sit or stand opposite each other and respond in the moment with a repeated phrase. This helps actors increase their listing skills and helps them to respond truthfully under imaginary circumstances. It breaks you down and builds you up. A few famous actors who've studied and use the Meisner Technique are, James Franco, Naomi Watts, James Gandolfini, Diane Keaton, Sandra Bullock, Timothee Chalamet, Sam Rockwell, Jack Nicholson, Robert Duval & so many more.

4) Stella Adler Technique – Developed her own version of the "Method". She was one of the few American actors to study directly with Stanislavsky. And she eventually cultivated her own technique. Her technique is a little different because she teaches to utilize your imagination in addition to emotional recall. Some say she married the "Meisner" and "Method" technique together. She once said, "drawing on the emotions I experienced, for example, when my mother died-to create a role is sick and schizophrenic. If that is acting, I don't want to do it." Adler believed actors should rely on their imaginations and doing external research rather than digging up traumatizing memories from their personal lives. She believes in artistic independence, action, script analysis and interpretation, imagination and staying true to humanity. A few famous actors who've studied and use the Stella Adler Technique are, Robert DeNiro, Benicio Del Toro, Marlon Brando, Harvey Keitel, Salma Hayek, Kevin Costner and many more.

5) The Chekhov Technique – Michael Chekhov was Stanislavski's favorite student and one of Russia's most brilliant actors. The Chekhov Technique marries the 1st step, which is the "inner life", which are the characters imagination, intellect and emotions and the 2nd step, which is to express this inner life with the body. The two coupled together are called "creative individuality" because the actor creates the life of the character through imagination and finds ways to express themselves as the character through physical movement. Some call it "Psycho-social" because the technique is based on the connection between the body and psychology. A few famous actors who've studied and use the Chekhov Technique are Anthony Hopkins, Clint Eastwood and more.

6) Practical Aesthetics – William H. Macy and David Mamet created an acting technique called "Practical Aesthetics" based on the teachings of Stanislavsky, Meisner and philosopher Epictetus. This Technique is made up of 4 steps. 1) Literal- The most basic description of what is happening in the scene. 2) Want- What does one character ultimately want the other character to say or do. 3)

Essential Action- what the actor wants in the scene and what they are doing. 4) As If- as if relates to the essential action and the actor's own life. For example: To make you love me "as if" you were my husband who left me for another woman. This puts the actor in an emotional real state and helps them to escape the fiction of the scene and plants them right into a memory that actually happened to create an even more heightened reality in the scene. A few famous actors who've studied and use the practical Aesthetics Technique are William H. Macy, Felicity Huffman, Rose Byrne, Jessica Alba, Camryn Manheim and more.

7) Substitution – Uta Hagen taught at a school I attended when I was 17 years old Herbert Berghof Studio (HB Studio) was the first acting school I attended. I would cut some of my high school classes or dart down to Bank Street directly after school to attend this class. I didn't have the pleasure to meet or be taught by Uta Hagen but I purchased, read and watched her DVD's and books "A Challenge for the Actor" & "Respect for Acting". Her technique teaches actors to substitute their own experiences and emotional recollections for the given circumstances in a scene. A few famous actors who've studied and use the Substitution or the "Transference" technique are Mathew Broderick, Sigourney Weaver, Debbie Allen, Susan Batson, Stockard Channing, Billy Crystal, Claire Danes, Drea de Matteo and many more.

> *"To be an interesting actor, you must be authentic. For you to ever be authentic, you must embrace who you really are. Do you have any idea how liberating it is to not care what people think about you? Well, that's what we're here to do."* –**Sanford Meisner**

> *"The actor has to develop his body. The actor has to work on his voice. But the most important thing the actor has to work on is his mind."* – **Stella Adler**

"That's what technique is. That's what craft is. It's not needing me anymore and knowing how to work and how to fix it when it's not working." –***Sanford Meisner***

Another Awesome way to study the craft of acting and surrounding yourself with amazing talent is to take Improv Classes. Improvising means to act, compose, speak or create without preparation. Improvisation is such an important tool for actors to be able to master or at least have good knowledge of. Mastering the art of improvisation helps actors think quicker, be more witty, be able to break a script down easier, see scripts in a 3 dimensional way, helps them develop characters easier, respond to their scene partners more truthfully and live more in the moment. It makes actors better listeners and helps actors create some of the best moments in film because sometimes a director and writer gives you the freedom to freestyle on set and go off the cuff while staying true to the story to see what magic will happen. Improv unlocks your creativity and wildest imagination and frees you and anyone else in your scene. Yes there are rules that you must follow and respect when it comes to learning and performing improv but these rules allow you to act and play at the highest level of your intelligence which can unlock the most exciting parts of your acting.

I have and still attend classes at UCB, The Upright Citizens Brigade. This school started as an improvisational and sketch comedy group that emerged from Chicago's improv Olympic that started in 1990 by Matt Besser, Amy Poehler, Ian Robert's, Matt Walsh, Adam McKay, Rick Roman, Horatio Sanz and drew Franklin. They have LA and New York City classes. This is probably one of the best classes I have ever taken in my entire life. Improv 101 scared the hell out of me but it was also life changing and cracked my brain open to an understanding of a new way and such a fun way of performing improv. Like I said there are rules to Improv and those rules allow you to set necessary boundaries and to not get lost and drown in an uncomfortable world of looking like you have no idea what you're doing and having an amazing time. This honestly helped me become a better communicator in life and even a better writer. I can now deal with people on a healthier, more honest, fun and witty way, which has totally raised the bar on my personality. I can talk with the best of them and not feel like I'm shriveling into the floor regardless of how influential, intelligent and superior someone or a group of people might believe they are. I hold my own around everyone and I truly owe it to improv classes at UCB.

For a list of Imrpov classes & Schools that I have either experienced personally and loved or heard great things about in New York & LA, visit theactorshustle.com for resources. Please remember to do your own research before making a commitment to any of my suggested resources. Make sure they are right for you.

"You must either modify your dreams or magnify your skills." - ***Jim Rohn***

"That thing that burns inside of you because you haven't done it and keeps you up at night. Just decide you're going to do it right now and stop at nothing until you complete It." - ***Shana Solomon***

"The smartest thing you can do is put every dollar you have towards your dreams and goals. Give yourself no excuses." - ***Shana Solomon***

IN ADDITION TO STUDYING THE CRAFT OF ACTING In order to surround YOURSELF WITH AWESOME ACTORS YOU CAN ALWAYS….

2) WATCH THE GREATS

Not only is it fun but it's also a form of studying when you watch the greats on TV, film and in live theatre. Please, I beg you to go see live theater as much as you can from small free and inexpensive black box theaters to Broadway shows because some of the material you will be studying and performing in class will be from the shows, films and theater pieces you watch. Once you start to audition you will notice that you will be auditioning for roles that will be on current TV shows and Theater. Shows like "Law & Order", "This Is Us", "Grey's Anatomy", "Blue Bloods", "High Maintenance", "The Waitress", "Chicago" and "The book of Mormon" have been running for years and are always looking for new talent.

Watching the greats also helps you to **STAY IN IT.** It's very important to constantly surround yourself with what you want to do in life and the more you surround yourself with other working, successful actors, weather it's in person, on TV, in the movie theaters or on stage, is the more your subconscious will start to pick up the habit of taking action towards your acting goals. You may also be inspired in many ways from watching the greats. When I saw John Leguizamo's "FREAK", "SEXAHOLIC" & "GHETTO KLOWN" on Broadway, it inspired me to write my own one woman show, 'The Closet Bitch' and perform it for the world. You never know what gems you might pick up from watching the greats.

Check these websites for lower priced tickets to Big shows on Broadway, off-Broadway and off-off Broadway shows in NYC, LA and many more cities.

- Goldstar.com
- Broadway .com
- Howtickets.com

- Theatermania.com
- Vividseats.com
- TDF.org
- Playbill.com

"How an actor truly learns is by watching and being surrounded by great actors. You instantly grow and your performance gets better and better." **-Shana Solomon**

"Sometimes we grow from experiencing and being inspired by someone else's magic. So why not surround yourself with magical experiences?" **–Shana Solomon**

Taking a leap of faith and surrounding yourself with great actors can happen by doing all of the above…

3) BUT WHAT ABOUT AUDITIONS?

An acting teacher once told me, "While you're in acting class, do not audition. Just focus on strengthening your craft to gain the confidence you need to walk in that audition room fully loaded and ready to kill it." But I say, do what you gotta do!

Do what your gut is telling you to do and listen to your spirit. Is it burning inside of you to audition right now, before or even during your acting class? Then by all means you go right on ahead and audition your heart out. I will say unless it's a paid, union job or you get the opportunity to work with some great quality talent, don't allow the audition or the gig take you out of your class and mastering your craft zone. It's totally okay to miss a few classes but if you love your class and are growing exponentially from it, figure out how to not miss so many classes and work around your class schedule. There are so many projects out there that aren't professional. So do your research on the director, producers, DP, writers and other actors on the project and try to only interrupt your class to work with people with great track records and experience in the film industry. This way you have a greater chance of not wasting your time or money.

Having tunnel vision while studying acting is one of the best things a new actor can do. It allows you to take the necessary time to learn and hone in on your craft and be fully present while in class. I have experienced both. While studying with Deena I did 2 years straight of learning, studying, homework & rehearsing for class performances at least 8 hours per week. I put in at least 20 hours per week into growing as an actor. That's damn near a part time job! I knew I was going to become a beast by the time I completed my training. And I did. I've also taken "method" acting classes to add new tools to my belt while I was a working actor. So I'd be on set one day and the other in class but I couldn't always be fully present. I'd be checking my phone for shooting schedules and updates, not showing up to class because my shoot date just so happened to fall on a class day, I disappointed my scene partner in class because after all of our rehearsal, I couldn't show up for our class performance because of my shooting schedule. But this can all be okay depending on what's most important to YOU. I booked a super important acting job and I wasn't going to cancel it for class. So I decided to re-take the class once my shooting was complete. And I did.

So how do you audition form where you are?

If you haven't ever auditioned in your life or have very little experience auditioning it's totally okay. There are actors who have taken a leap of faith and nailed it on the first try. But I would suggest you prepare yourself as much as possible for the win by knowing the character your auditioning for, the tone of the script and or scene, and what the objective of the character is. Also, being off book is super important. There's nothing like going into a room and having the confidence that you know your lines and know what the character is talking about and what they want. If you need help with your auditioning technique I would also take an auditioning technique class. You can find some really great auditioning technique classes at actorsconnection.com, theactrosgreenroom.com, oneononenyc.com or oneononela.com in addition to many awesome auditioning coaches out there which can also be found on Theactorshustle.com for more resources.

Now I don't want to encourage everybody to just ditch the idea of taking an acting class and go straight to auditioning by any means. I just know there are a few select actors out there who know they can kill an audition because they already have the confidence, chops and are perfect for the role. But even if you book that audition, keep in mind that the day may come when you will need to up your game and will feel the need to jump into a class, or get an acting coach to strengthen those acting muscles and chops and learn some technique.

I strongly believe in whatever works for you, works for you.

The key to booking roles is to always be prepared and no matter what happens in that auditioning room you let it go when you walk out because at that point it is all up to them to decide. You've already done the work and all that you could do. It's also a numbers game. The more you audition, the more you will become a pro at auditioning and the more you will book! I auditioned my ass off when I first started out. I still do. I have sucked big time in the auditioning room and I have also slayed many. I used to beat myself up about the ones I didn't book. But for some reason it always worked out because I always managed to book the roles that were perfect for ME. You never know what the universe has in store for you, so never hold your head down for a role that you don't book because **YOUR TIME WILL COME IF YOU KEEP GOING.**

There are a number of websites and publications that you can subscribe to in order to find non-union and union auditions such as..

ActorsAccess.com - This is a very popular one and one of the sites I subscribed to and used daily when I first started out. I got tons of auditions from using it and booked my first paid role! It is a subscription-based site where you create a profile with your headshot, resume and reel. You have to pay a monthly fee but I'd say it's totally worth it. Casting directors, production companies and industry professionals will see your profile. You also get to see what's being cast in other areas of the US and it has lots of industry info on the site. USE THIS SITE TO YOUR ADVANTAGE! IT'S QUITE AWESOME.

Backstage.com – I used this site as well. It's similar to actorsaccess but it doesn't have anywhere near as many auditions. They primarily focus on theater. Where this site wins is that it has lots of helpful industry tips, interviews and info for actors to learn and grow from. I would soak up as much helpful content as you can from this site.

Mandy.com – Another subscription based website that has jobs for actors, directors and more. I've booked a few non-paid acting jobs from here when I first started out which helped build my reel.

There are also a few Facebook pages and IG accounts that post casting information frequently. You can find them here:

FB

IG

Here is a little bonus I put together for you In case you have an audition coming up!

Here are 20 Quick Audition Tips to help you crush your audition!

1. Read all of the information you receive about your upcoming audition in the email or post (who is the writer, director, Producer? Is this a union project? When and what time is the audition? Who is already cast? What studio, network is this

for? When does the job start and end? What additional info did they include in the email/post? What is your character breakdown telling you about your character? Read the other character breakdowns as well. This can reveal more information about your character and the environment. Read the entire script if it's provided for clues and a full understanding of the story being told and how your character fits in and why they are important to the story. Also, read your audition material at least 10 times to truly understand what's going on. We miss a lot from only reading things once or twice. Pay attention to the details here.

2. Ask yourself, "What is going on in this scene? Where am I and how does this make me feel? Am I nervous? Cold? Squinting from sunlight? Happy? In love?

3. Ask yourself "who is my character and what does my character want more than anything in this scene/script and what is he/she doing or willing to do to get it? The breakdown and scene or script usually gives you all of this info including. If not, you should create this on your own. Is she bubbly? Awkward? Is she a siren? A detective? How does she move? Does she have a wall up and if so why? If there isn't a back-story on your character, give them one that makes sense to you. Write a small journal entry to tap into your creativity and who your character might be. What are your characters goals?

4. Who is your character talking to and or about in this scene? This is super important as it sets the tone of the conversation and mood of the scene. If you're talking to your grandmother even if you get angry, you probably won't be yelling at the top of your lungs. Instead you'll restrain yourself but maybe try to leave or break free from the conversation or change the subject, which lets you know your character has a bit of an inner struggle.

5. Now that you know these things about who your character is, what they want in this scene and where they are and what their relationship is to the person/people in the scene or being mentioned in the scene, it's time to make some choices by connecting each "want" your character has to an "action". I use this amazing book called "Actions: The Actors Thesaurus" By: Marina Calderone. It's one of my best weapons for when I'm stuck or need to find a verb that sparks my mind and basically inspires me to take a specific action for auditions and even when I'm on set. There might come a time when you may say to yourself "what is my character doing when she/he says this? All you have to do is ask yourself a basic question like "what is my character doing here?" If your character is trying to get information out of a suspect, you might look up the word "Question" in the book and it will give you many different actions your character can take to question someone to gather info from the other character. Like seductively question, jokingly question, passively aggressively question or carefully question, probe, quiz or interrogate someone. This way your character can have layers and colors and not feel flat when they're asking the other character in the scene multiple questions. In real life when we're questioning someone and we're trying to get an answer out of them or get what we want, we ask questions in many different ways even if it's the same question. We might start off sweet, child like and playful and then start becoming annoying then we start begging and then we might start to question in a more aggressive and serious tone. That's what I mean by colors and layers. Choose actions that build and make sense to the tone of the scene and character. Now you've got somewhere to go.

6. Who is she talking to and what is there relationship? Always be super clear.

7. Memorize the audition material (all of your lines in the scene that you will be auditioning).

8. Once memorized really get it into your bones by creating movement while saying your lines like do jumping jacks or throw a pillow up in the air and catch it until you have said all of your lines in the auditioning material. This helps you not get thrown off and most of all you will be able to live in the moment during your audition. You will most likely have your lines down packed if you do this.

9. Start to make some choices. Maybe it's how you say a line or a pair of glasses you decide to wear or an outfit you put on to create your character's look (keep this simple), find the funny and make light of a dark and sinister moment to make your character even more intense or scary and possibly do the opposite for a kind and lighthearted character. Play with what your character could be doing in the material but make sure it makes sense. The Actions book I mentioned will help you and inspire you to make some amazing choices. Always remember you can't play angry. We as humans get angry when we feel uncomfortable, disrespected, let down, hurt and cheated but you can't just be an angry character without connecting to why you are angry and upset. Also when we're angry we don't always yell. Yes sometimes yelling is super appropriate but remember when you're auditioning, most actors will choose the obvious easy choice of yelling because the character seems angry. If you believe there are other ways, colors and layers you can add to your characters actions other than yelling at the top of your lungs to show how angry your character is, please take that beautiful well thought out risk. Always try not to be typical because these casting directors see sometimes hundreds of people for a role and hope that YOU will show them something different. Anger is sometimes quiet or manipulative or even passive aggressive. Whatever you choose please make sure it makes sense to the scene and

the objective of your character. Don't decide to be different just to be different. Be different because you did the work it took to find the interesting layers of your character.

10. Find your moment before the scene started. What was your character and even the other characters doing before the moment begins in your auditioning material? For example: if the scene or script starts off with a couple arguing at home maybe they were just in the car talking about whatever they're arguing about or just making love or just eating or waking up and there was quiet tension between them or even laughter that eventually got taken out of context. Look at the time of day, where the scene is taking place, what the characters are wearing, how they are speaking to one another, I mean look at every detail to help determine what your moment before was so when you go into the audition room you can have that pre moment for yourself before you start which will help you create more of an internal story and make your character more human and relatable.

*You should now be super clear on what your "Character Container" is. A character container is the character you have created based on the information you have been given paired with who you are, your imagination and who believe this character to be.

11. Perform the scene at least 10 times as the character before your audition. Do this with your choices, character container, sense of location and the other characters in the scene and actions that will tell the story in your audition material. You can do this alone or with someone who is willing to read the other character(s) in the scene with you. Just be sure you're having a real conversation. No actors tone here. In life we speak for a reason and sound like normal human beings regardless of how abnormal we can be. Make sure you check in with self and don't do that raised weird "actors" pitch at the

end of your sentences. If you need help with sounding like you're having a real conversation while saying your lines and know you need to be more authentic, you should say something aloud to yourself about how your day went yesterday and then at some point allow the lines from your scene just flow right in. Don't take a break and do not pause from speaking about your real life personal story when you go into your character lines. Allow them to flow right into each other almost as if it was the story continuing. If you notice the inflection or tone of your voice changed too much into this fake acting voice, then start over until you sound pretty much just like how you sounded when you talked about how your day went yesterday. If you need to record yourself to hear yourself you can do this on just about any smart phone. Do this and you will be well on your way to sounding like some of your favorite big actors and will get further along in your career.

12. Have your headshot and resume with you unless you or your rep (agent/manager) has emailed it to them.

13. Show up 10-15 minutes before your audition appointment. You might run into a slow elevator or have to use the bathroom. There's no room for tardiness. And never be that creepy early actor who's there an hour before the audition. That's just too much.

14. Breathe. Close your eyes and take 10 deep breaths, go in the bathroom and do this if you have to but do this to help alleviate any anxiety you may have. I usually do yoga that morning after exercising. After you breathe, visualize you going in that audition room and everything working to your advantage. See yourself crushing it from beginning to end and see the casting directors heads nod, smile and or be wowed with a very positive reaction.

15. Prepare yourself anyway you feel you need to. Maybe you need to go over any lines, or find your moment before. Just don't be so in your head about your moment before that you walk into the audition room in a state where you can't even say hello or respond to what the casting director is saying. But as soon as you take you place in front of that audition camera, get into it. Breathe some more if you have to.

16. When you walk into the room, greet everyone as you would a room full of cool people whom you respect. Everyone in that room wants you to succeed and hopes you make their jobs easy by crushing it and being the actor they cast. So go ahead and own your power and be yourself. Start off by saying "Hey Guys!" or "Hi!" or "Hello, how's it going?" and close the door being you if need be. If they ask you any questions don't be afraid to answer them and talk to them as you would any cool person. Let it flow.

17. If casting hasn't told you yet, ask where should you stand, sit and who will you be reading with if it isn't obvious to you. I do this all the time. You need to be clear on how to move before you move.

18. Trust yourself and do the work you came to do including your choices.

19. Say "good bye, have a great day and thank you". If they say or ask you anything else, again talk to them and let it flow. No pressure here, your work is done. Leave the room.

20. Let it all go! You've done all you came to do. And if you messed up, it's okay. There will be tons of other auditions for you to do amazing on. Life is full of lessons so this may be one of them. Don't beat yourself up. Tell yourself you did your best under the circumstances and you're living the dream because guess what? You got a chance to act today! So, work

on what needs to be worked on moving forward but you must let that audition go.

"You can't, won't and shouldn't please everybody. That would mean you don't have an opinion of your own. Just be who you are, you're the only one who can." -**Shana Solomon**

"I used to hate auditions. But then I realized sometimes that audition is the only opportunity I have to act that day or week. So now I just do the work and prepare so I can have a ball and appreciate that one moment I get to do what I love to do." - **Shana Solomon**

Before we move onto chapter 2 I really need you to understand something super important as an actor. This is probably the most important thing to learn outside of technique.

An actor is a **PRODUCT**. Yes of course you are a human being but the Television, Film & theater world is the entertainment BUSINESS and all BUSINESSES are concerned with making money from buying and selling products and or services. So you my love are a beautiful product, some in the industry call it a "BRAND" and you must decide what your brand is and sell the shit out of it every chance you get! You are your own business and the product you are selling to casting directors, producers, writers, directors is YOU, YOUR LOOK & YOUR TALENT (Whatever you are great at doing mixed with your personality and style) So it's very important to know who you are and what your thing is and what comes natural to you. Also how do you want the world to perceive you?

For the longest I didn't know who I was let alone what type of product I was as an actor because to me, I am so many things but then the more I let go and realized the types of roles I connected to, what I wanted to say as an actor, how I wanted to use my platform as an actor, what types of scripts speak to me in connection with who I am around and what I stand for, I realized I am the strong, positive, takes no prisoners, firecracker, game-changer, leading lady in a comedy, drama, franchise film, character actor who never takes her clothes off for any dollar amount and empowers women. Not saying I haven't played a prostitute or a crack-head or a down and out type of role, but I've never been naked on screen. And this is no shade or judgment towards anyone who's okay with being nude on screen but it's just not my thing. But as far as playing characters that don't appear to be strong, I give them all back-stories to add layers and colors to be able to relate to them in order to understand them and always find what they were once fighting for or what they are currently fighting for. We all have weak moments in life. I usually say maybe this is my characters weak moment but she will rise again or has already used her strength before this moment and has no more fight left in her but she was once strong. To me, they are all strong women at some point in their lives. Some of these roles were also to get my foot in the door to learn the ropes and create relationships and build TV or film credits. But I never waved my morals for a role or a dollar. My Product is, I am a leading Lady & a character Actor who has Transparent, Vulnerable, Sexy, Firecracker, nurturing, Strength. BOOM! Similar to a Rita Hayworth, Regina King, Jada Pinkett-Smith, Julia Roberts, Phylicia Rashad, Natalie Portman, Helena Bonham Carter, Meryl Streep, Viola Davis & Frances McDormand.

So Know Your product and those casting you and offering you roles will be clearer on the type of roles and scripts that are for you and casting you will be easier.

Now I want to be clear on the difference between brand and type or "type cast".

A brand is a specific look, vibe and feeling you get when you think of a product or person. Take the Apple brand, Chanel or Lady Gaga for example. If each of them were to come out with a new product, we all would have a similar idea of the look, vibe and feeling that product would have but they can also even sometimes surprise us while keeping on brand. For example, Apple will always drop a new super sleek and clean device that solves a new problem we never thought existed making our lives easier. But they also went left in a great way and decided to sell Beats headphones along with their products. Chanel would come out with a bag or a new line for the season that has a chic classic timeless feminine look and vibe but sometimes they might add vibrant street wear and colors to connect with today's fashion forward culture. Lady Gaga, weather its music or wardrobe or any kind of art, well we'd expect her to do something she hasn't done before, wild, edgy and full of imagination. But even when she did 'A Star Is Born', most people considered her to be "normal" in my opinion a great way of course because she did fantastic but there were no crazy wild outfits and hair which was super different for Gaga. But it still stayed on brand because she surprised us as she always does. But when you're "type cast" as an actor...it pigeon holds the actor into a specific type of role that you might never see them get out of EVER. Unless they break themselves out of the box...

Example of an actor who is a Brand: Margot Robbie is a beautiful, sexy, delicate, powerful, spicy, Australian leading lady who mostly plays the role of the beautiful and sometimes wild and crazy love interest but in the movie "I, TONYA" she jumped right into a character and became Tonya Harding, who's depicted in the movie as a trailer trash, unattractive, beer guzzling 80's hair rocking ice skater with some serious childhood issues. Margot played Tonya Harding beautifully and can and is still recognized for her brand. However if she only played roles of the beautiful love interest or the hot girl over and over again, people might label her as being "type cast" and May get tired of seeing her play the same "type" of character. But now I believe casting directors can see her playing many different roles all within respect to her brand. To me, that's the true definition of an actor with a brand.

"The Rock" Is a brand but he's also a super specific "type". He's a tough gentle, loving, handsome, gun toting, wrestling action hero, and leading man, solid as steel, body builder, smart jock that can't be beat. He gets roles because of his brand and I think it's fantastic. When producers want an action hero or a leading man who's a big, sweet, tough guy they call the rock! But if he wanted to play the role of a sensitive and timid nerd or a sweet dad with absolutely no fighting and gun toting involved, I think he can do it. It would probably be really funny and interesting to see. Would the world be ready for it? I don't know but I'd watch it because the rock constantly improves and reinvents himself. So weather you may think he's a brand or type cast, that man uses his brains and his determination to play super smart in the business of acting and does both seamlessly and delivers high level performances.

A very well known actor who most people consider being type cast once said to me, "I may be type cast but at least I'm **always** CAST." I actually loved her for saying that. And by **always** being cast she **always** made money and **always** made connections and always stays relevant. She networked her but off and now she's producing her own films. One of which is currently on NETFLIX. And guess what?? She cast herself in her own film and made sure she didn't play her "Type". Such a smart move and a smart woman.

So being type cast isn't necessarily a bad thing. It just all depends on what you want and what you do with your opportunities.

*"Never allow yourself to be boxed in. Speak up, work, and fight for the roles you want. You deserve to spread your wings and fly." -***Shana Solomon**

*"Decide who you want to be and how you will do it. But be so prepared that whatever comes your way doesn't knock you off track permanently it only takes you on another road to the same destination." –***Shana Solomon**

How to discover your product/or Brand??

Some of you may already have the answer to this question. You might say I'm the tough, silent good looking no nonsense leading man in action thriller films and television series roles. If you know this, your headshots and reel and photos on your social media and most of your marketing material should reflect this look and vibe. This however doesn't mean every photo you take should be in a leather jacket holding a gun and a hand grenade with a 5 o'clock shadow or beard. But some of it can. It's important to highlight that "thing" about you that sets you apart and is UNDENIABLE. So showcase all sides of you but focus on what's undeniable.

If you don't know the UNDENIABLE qualities and characteristics about yourself do not panic. Ask 5 of your friends, co-workers, family or 5 people that really know you right now, "what is undeniable about me?" "If you were casting a movie, what type of role would you cast me as?", "What character in a movie or TV show that you have seen reminds you of me?", "What are some of my best obvious qualities about me?" "What kind of look do you think I have?" "What would you say my type is when it comes to my look and personality?" Write the most common UNDENIABLE qualities that were said from the people you asked here:

_____
_____
_____
_____
_____
_____
_____
_____
_____
_____

If you are still unclear and or have nobody to ask then ask yourself these questions. Try to steer away from saying and thinking you can play every character. This is not an exercise to see how versatile or talented you are. This is an exercise to define your "BRAND/PRODUCT" to determine as to how you will market yourself to make casting you easy. That is it. And I want you to be honest with yourself. If you are a bit awkward and have heard people call you a geek or nerd then wonderful! Own it! This might be your beautiful undeniable quality. Don't shy away from it or allow these titles to make you feel like you're being held back or put you in a box. This "title" will be the thing that will do the exact opposite. If you get cast as a nerdy scientist in a marvel film and are making $160,000 per year then ride that amazing wave until you decide to hire a personal trainer and then buy a few amazing pieces for your wardrobe that gives you the new look you want to be recognized as and hire an amazing photographer to capture that look, post it all over your social media and website and market the hell out of the NEW YOU! By then you will have grown as an actor got your foot in the door, have respect and a name and now other doors will automatically open for you. This acting world is a hustle but you have to know how to hustle and do what works for YOU! This is how you kick down a small easy door to get to a big door that will become easier to kick down if you follow the path of least resistance. And that path starts with you being super clear on your **UNDENIABLE QUALITY**, which is your **Product** or **BRAND**. I want you to market that with the monologues, scenes, headshots, looks you choose and even how you dress when you attend meet and greets and auditions.

"Good things happen to those who hustle" – ***Anais Nin***

2

The Hustle

Yup, I'm getting right into it!

So now that you've gotten some acting and auditioning technique under your belt or are just super ready and confident to get out there, allow me to give you..

THE HUSTLE

Here is what you will need

THE 7 MUST HAVE HUSTLE TOOLS FOR ACTORS

1. Headshots
2. Acting Resume
3. Acting Reel
4. Social Media & Website

5. A Printer/Print shop close by you or audition location

6. The "In's" (Any website, publication, event, group or class that gives you info on upcoming auditions, meet and greets or how to connect with casting directors, directors and producers that would be interested in you for current castings like actorsaccess.com.

7. The Most Important and my favorite – A go getter, positive kickass attitude that can take a 'No' like a champ takes blow to the chin and keeps on getting up and fighting for the win.

HEADSHOTS

Headshots are super duper important!!! Headshots are for the casting team to see what you look like and decide weather or not your look fits the role they're casting prior to your audition. If a casting director, your agent or manager or anyone in the industry sends you an audition, it's usually because they are interested in your look and would like to see you audition or play the role.

It's incredibly important that you look like YOU in your headshots. However you would walk in an audition room on any random day looking and feeling great, that is how you should look in your headshots. If you want to wear some makeup, do you. Just don't go overboard because you think this is glamour time. This is, show them who you are at your best without over doing it time. So show off your product/brand!

How many looks do you need?

It's always best to have a minimum of 2 types of headshots. A dramatic headshot or what I like to call a relaxed or serious look for those dramatic roles and a commercial look where you're happy and smiling from the inside out for comedic roles. It's all in the eyes so make sure you prepare for your shoot by drinking lots of water a few days before, go light on the sodium to reduce bloating, get a good nights sleep the night before, choose your favorite clothing to wear a ahead of time so your not freaking out the night before and are able to purchase or put together the looks you want, show up on time, breathe and relax while shooting and leave the rest up to the photographer.

How to choose a great headshot photographer?

I used to freak out about this but honestly it's all about your budget and then looking at just a few photographers portfolios that you think are amazing who shoot the way you would like to be shot. If you want to be shot in natural light by the water in Brooklyn then find a photographer who does just that. If you want a more studio look with a backdrop using a fan to create that Beyoncé blowing performance hair then go with a photographer who does exactly that! Like I said before, do you!

For a list of amazing photographers that I have either experienced personally, enjoyed working with and have me great headshots or heard great things about other than Pete Lott and David Noles in New York, Emily Lambert in LA, Brian Jones in GA & Noel Marcantel in New Orleans, visit theactorshustle.com for more resources. Please remember to do your own research before making a commitment to any of my suggested resources. Make sure they are right for you. Just make sure you look like YOU.

Back in the day, like 10+ years ago, we had to print out like 250+ copies of your 8x10 sized headshot at a quality print shop like REPRODUCTIONS to give to CD's every time you auditioned as well as use them for mailings or drop offs at agency's to be considered but you should only start out with like 50-100 copies now because you will be mainly emailing your headshots or posting them on your online profiles for services like IMBDPro.com (online database of information related to films, television, home videos, and video games, and internet streams, including cast, production crew and personnel biographies, plot summary's, trivia & fan reviews) and websites like actorsaccess.com. But you will be handing them out at theater auditions and most likely non-Union auditions and meet and greets. So when you go to reproductions (www.reproductions.com) or any quality headshot/photo print shop to do quality touch up's and edit and print your headshots (which I suggest you do unless your photographer is amazing at editing as well) be sure to ask them for an edited emailable (I made that word up) headshot file which usually comes in a .png or .jpeg format. Reproductions are also really great for printing out headshots. Their quality is undeniable.

Every artist is a walking business. Your marketing tools are your headshots and your reel. That's what people see that's what your out there pushing trying to get a rep and that isn't easy. - **Jay Ellis**

RESUME

When you don't have any acting experience it can be a little discouraging to even think of creating an actors resume. But here's the thing, it doesn't matter, just start from where you are. The first person that books you will be booking you because you killed it in that audition room not because your resume is flooded with TV network & studio film credits. Most auditions that actors get in the beginning are non-union and non-paid, low budget, or modified low budget, student and short films and non-equity, non-paid theater roles. So the casting directors on these projects aren't expecting your resume to be lit up with credentials from TV, big budget films and Broadway. Even if you had major roles all over your resume and you did absolutely terrible on your audition, do you think the casting director is going to say, "well even though she was absolutely terrible she was on Law & Order so let's just book her because she worked with Marishka Hagarty". Nah, that's most likely not ever going to happen. So don't worry, beyond this sentence about what credits and experience you don't have. You wanna know what I put on my resume when I first started out? My name, phone number, a play I did in high school (but of course I made it look like it was a theater gig) all of the one acts I studied and performed in front of my acting class, my college experience and my skills, like Bartending, billiards (I'm a mean pool shark) and my outlandish ridiculous contagious laugh. That's it!

Here's one of my first resumes that my beautiful mother helped me with after attending the Deena Levy Theater Studio and started on my auditioning journey:

Shana A. Solomon
AFTRA
EMAIL WENT HERE

Eyes: Dark Brown   Hair: Black

Height: 5ft; Weight: 105lbs

THEATRE

Four Dogs And A Bone	Collette	Producer's Club, NY
21	Boo	Theatre 54 @ Shelter Studios, NY
Savage in Limbo	Linda Rotunda	Producer's Club, NY
Romeo & Juliet	Juliet	Deena Levy Theatre Studio
Fallen Angels	Julia	Deena Levy Theatre Studio
A Hatful Of Rain	Celia	Deena Levy Theatre Studio
Women of Manhattan	Judy	Deena Levy Theatre Studio
The Heidi Chronicles	Heidi	Deena Levy Theatre Studio
Marvin's Room	Bessie	Deena Levy Theatre Studio
Straight Drama	Carmen/Supporting	Tribeca PAC, NY

TRAINING

Scene Study	Deena Levy	Deena Levy Theatre Studio
Meisner Technique	Deena Levy	Deena Levy Theatre Studio
Growtowski Integration	Deena Levy	Deena Levy Theatre Studio
Improvisation, Comedy	Jay Rhoderick, Don Puglisi	Deena Levy Theatre Studio
Movement	Deena Levy	Deena Levy Theatre Studio
Uta Hagen Technique	Deena Levy	Deena Levy Theatre Studio
Shakespeare	Deena Levy	Deena Levy Theatre Studio
Voice and Speech	Louis Colaianni	Deena Levy Theatre Studio
On-Camera	Peter Milner	T. Schreiber Studio, NY
Audition for Commercials	Terry Berland	Deena Levy Theatre Studio
Ivana Chubbuck Technique	Tasha Smith	Tasha Smith Actors Workshop

SPECIAL SKILLS

Improvisation, Outlandish Laugh, Comedic Timing, Munchkin Voice, Hip Hop and Freestyle Dancer; Italian, British, Southern & Spanish Dialects. Sales Management, Events Coordinator, Business Co-owner, Bartender, Billiards Player, Computer Skills, Travel, Athletic. Valid United States Passport.

COMMERCIALS: List Upon Request

After doing some background work on "All My Children", and "As The World Turns" and getting upgraded to having a line or two (which is considered an "Under 5 " role or being featured on set, which is when they show more of you throughout the scene and or you are asked to come back as staple background, I was able to put that as experience on my resume.

Shana A. Solomon
AFTRA
EMAIL WENT HERE

Eyes: Dark Brown　　　　　　　　　　　　　　　　　　　　　　　Hair: Black
　　　　　　　　　　　　　　　　　　　　　　　　　　Height: 5ft; Weight: 105lbs

THEATRE

Four Dogs And A Bone	Collette	Producer's Club, NY
21	Boo	Theatre 54 @ Shelter Studios, NY
Savage in Limbo	Linda Rotunda	Producer's Club, NY
Romeo & Juliet	Juliet	Deena Levy Theatre Studio
Fallen Angels	Julia	Deena Levy Theatre Studio
A Hatful Of Rain	Celia	Deena Levy Theatre Studio
Women of Manhattan	Judy	Deena Levy Theatre Studio
The Heidi Chronicles	Heidi	Deena Levy Theatre Studio
Marvin's Room	Bessie	Deena Levy Theatre Studio
Straight Drama	Carmen/Supporting	Tribeca PAC, NY

FILM/TELEVISION

All My Children	Patron	ABC, NY
As The World Turns	Patron	CBS, NY
The Baby Shower	Alanna/Supporting	NYU/Christie Colaprico, Dir.
When "MySpace" Goes Wrong	Chante/Lead	Serge Leonidas, Dir., NY
Selling Cute	Host	Serge Leonidas, Dir., NY

TRAINING

Scene Study	Deena Levy	Deena Levy Theatre Studio
Meisner Technique	Deena Levy	Deena Levy Theatre Studio
Growtowski Integration	Deena Levy	Deena Levy Theatre Studio
Improvisation, Comedy	Jay Rhoderick, Don Puglisi	Deena Levy Theatre Studio
Movement	Deena Levy	Deena Levy Theatre Studio
Uta Hagen Technique	Deena Levy	Deena Levy Theatre Studio
Shakespeare	Deena Levy	Deena Levy Theatre Studio

Voice and Speech	Louis Colaianni	Deena Levy Theatre Studio
On-Camera	Peter Milner	T. Schreiber Studio, NY
Audition for Commercials	Terry Berland	Deena Levy Theatre Studio
Ivana Chubbuck Technique	Tasha Smith	Tasha Smith Actors Workshop

SPECIAL SKILLS

Improvisation, Outlandish Laugh, Comedic Timing, Munchkin Voice, Hip Hop and Freestyle Dancer; Italian, British, Southern & Spanish Dialects. Sales Management, Events Coordinator, Business Co-owner, Bartender, Billiards Player, Computer Skills, Travel, Athletic. Valid United States Passport.

COMMERCIALS: List Upon Request

Also, my friend Serge who was an aspiring director and cinematographer wanted to shoot some content I'd written to stay busy and creative. I played all of the characters so I wouldn't have to depend on anybody but us. It was called "When MySpace Goes Wrong". This was back in 2009 when I think MySpace was still a thing. We got it done and Serge edited it to perfection. And I put that right on my resume, and why not? It was more acting experience.

But do you see how many credits I have listed on my resume from school? Almost every credit is from the one-act performances I had either done in Deena's class or performed during the Deena Levy Theater Studios showcase. And I proudly handed this resume out at auditions, to agents, casting directors and anyone else I felt needed to see my credentials.

Never feel inadequate for where you are. Especially if you're just starting out in this business. This is a journey, not a race so enjoy every beautiful moment knowing you have made progress and will continue to make progress but right here, right now is something special because you will never again be in this very moment.

The Actors Hustle

Shana A. Solomon

SAG-AFTRA~ AEA

www.ShanaSolomon.com

Hair: Black; Eyes: Dark Brown
Height: 5ft.; Weight: 105 lbs.

TELEVISION

Law & Order S/15	Co-Starring	NBC
All My Children	Feature	ABC
As the World Turns	Feature	CBS

FILM

Peanut Butter & Jelly	Supporting	David Winkfield, Director
ASA	Supporting	Sela Films; Michael Chahade, Director
Shadowboxing	Supporting	Breadth Films; Joshua Durham, Director
Cool Kidz	Lead	Red Wall Productions; Rosalyn Coleman, Dir.
Paramour	Lead	Maba Ba Productions
I Am a Fat Cat	Lead	Backseat Conceptions
Noah Dreams of Origami Fortunes	Supporting	Royce Dunnmore, Director, NYU

MUSIC & VIDEO

Fantasia: I'm Doing Me	Featured Dancer	Benny Boom, Director

THEATRE

The Closet Bitch	Shana and 12 Characters	C.O.W. Theater (One-Woman Show)
Four Dogs and A Bone	Collette	Producer's Club
IFNY Monologue Slam	Winner	Kumble Theater @ LIU
21	Boo	Theatre 54
Straight Drama	Carmen/Supporting	Tribeca PAC, NY
Romeo & Juliet	Juliet	Theatre 54
Richard III	Lady Anne	Producer's Club

EDUCATION & TRAINING

Deena Levy Theatre Studio (3 years)- NY, NY; Lehman College- Bronx, NY; Black Nexxus-NY, NY

Acting/Scene Study	Deena Levy, Marishka Phillips, Brette Goldstein, Rosalyn Coleman Williams, Tony Greco
Improvisation	Jay Rhoderick, Don Puglisi
On Camera	Terry Berland, Barry Shapiro, Judy Henderson, Brette Goldstein
Voice & Speech	Louis Colaianni
Dance	Footloose, Yoshi, Eric Negron, Chuck Davis

SPECIAL SKILLS

Improvisation, Outlandish Laugh, Comedic Timing, Character Voices, Athletic, Billiards, Teleprompter.
Dance: Hip Hop, Jazz, Freestyle, African, Merengue, Bachata, Pole Dancing.
Physical: Running, Weight Lifting, Firearms, Archery, Stage Combat & Fight Choreography.
Dialects: New York, Southern, Spanish, African, Patios, Italian, British, Valley Girl.
Valid U.S. Passport. Valid Drivers License. Willing to travel. Commercials upon request.

I booked my first paid short film "I Am A Fat Cat", on actorsaccess.com with that 1st beautiful makeshift resume. You have to "ACT AS IF" UNTIL YOU SUCCEED! If you believe that you are already a star then you are! That's all you need in addition to being prepared to make the people in the audition room see you shine. The resume has nothing to do with making them believe or disbelieve. Trust me on this one. It's just a piece of information they use to see what you have done. It's not meant to be used to judge you. And if they do, send them good vibes and thank the universe you didn't work with a self-centered asshole. Most of the casting directors in this industry want you to win and hope you are 'the one' when you walk through their doors. They want you to make their lives easier by doing a great job so they can cast the project and fulfill their jobs so just focus on the character you are playing and the characters objective and let your self-belief and skills shine.

My 3rd resume had a few cool credits on there. After booking that short film I mentioned, I started to book more and more work. The more work I booked, the more I removed the credits from Deena's class and replaced them with credits from films, commercials and TV.

You will start to see that little by little you will grow like a beautiful flower so enjoy the sunshine and the rain that life and this industry brings because they are both necessary to your growth.

How do I create my resume?

8. Your resume must be stapled and fit perfectly on the back of your 8x10 headshot when you hand them out at auditions and meet and greets. You can use Microsoft Word to create it. Use their Resume templates or find one online.

9. All of your information on your resume should always fit on one sheet of paper.

10. Make it super clean with an easy to read font. Also leave white space and don't cram too much info onto the resume. You don't have to list every single thing you did in school. Keep it simple by putting your contact info including name,

phone number, email, your union status (Equity/AEA, Sag-AFTRA, Sag-AFTRA Eligible or Non-Union) your height, weight, eye color, hair color and DO NOT put your age. Only put your age if you are under 18. Also, list your most important credits that you are proud of by breaking them down into sections (Theater, television, film, education and skills). You should put your agents or managers contact information if you have an exclusive agreement with them instead of your personal contact information. Do not put your address on your resume ever. There are too many creepy people in this world to just hand that information over.

11. Your Television, film and theatrical resume should state 'commercials upon request' at the bottom of the resume if you have commercial credits unless you need those credits to fill up space on your resume.

12. Do not put background work on your resume unless you were bumped up to a speaking role, which is basically a co-star role or under-5 role (a role where you have under 5 speaking lines).

13. Never ever lie on your resume! Everybody knows somebody in this industry and it's a reeaaaaaly small circle so be very careful about lying on your resume and even in person about what you have done or what you will be doing.

Google "actor's resume" and look at the links and images that pop up and look at the different types of resumes so you can get even more of an idea as to what style suits you and be inspired to create your own.

"Invest in your dreams, grind now, shine later." -**Unknown**

REEL

Your reel is basically your commercial. It's advertising you as the product and how amazing you are.

The purpose of your actor's reel is to create an emotional response that encourages casting directors and anyone else in the industry who is apart of the casting process to bring you in for an audition, for agents and managers to see if they're interested in representing you, for a producer to hire you and of course to show the world your skills, talent and work ethic. Your actor's reel shows your work and credits to raise awareness on you as a brand. You are basically convincing viewers that you, the featured product, are the one they should spend their money on. It needs to be quick, impactful and to the point. Your reel should have scenes that clearly identify you as the actor. There should never be any confusion as to whose reel it is. You are the only actor who should be shining!

Your reel should be 1-3 minutes long. If it's longer, it better be damn good. Remember, a lot of people have the attention span (as my fiancé likes to say about me) of a Nail.

It's good to have 2-5 scenes on your reel. You can also have 1 really strong scene for your reel or more than 5. Just make sure it's either crazy funny or really powerful and emotionally ON! Always put your best scene first. You can also include a montage (super short clips of you with no talking while an amazing song that hypes up your product plays). But keep your montage to about 15 seconds.

Once your reel is done, it should go everywhere! YouTube, Vimeo, Your website, All of your social media and your profiles on all of the industry sites you subscribe to like actorsaccess.com and IMDB.com My reason for this is because you want to promote it as much as possible. You never know who might see it and ask you to audition or offer you a role from seeing your reel.

Check out these links to a few of my reels:

My earlier reel:

https://m.youtube.com/watch?v=ESxftw5zpbo

My reel from a few years ago:

https://vimeo.com/255951226

But what if I don't have any footage for a reel?????

Now we all want that killer reel that has quality, well shot scenes with the most perfect sound and lighting capturing us in stellar roles with the best lines and all the shine from professional productions such as feature films and network television. Buuuuuuut we don't always have that type of footage when we're ready to do a reel and that's perfectly freaking okay, because you can always create it.

New actors and actors with little to no footage of themselves in a quality production should do a few things to build their reel.

1) Shoot and edit a scene(s) or a monologue(s) yourself

You can save a ton of money and also gain some confidence in filming yourself with your phone (make sure the video quality is good) or if you happen to have a good quality camera that shoots great video like a Sony, canon or a Nikon. Also make sure you have a tripod or something to hold your camera/phone in place and steady while you shoot. I really dig amazon because for the most part their prices are super reasonable when it comes to little gadgets like this. I've also splurged at B&H for a professional quality camera and tripod. It all depends on what works best for you.

Make sure you have great lighting and either a clean or nice background. You can film in your apartment or at a free location where there is natural light coming in from the windows. I love how natural light looks on camera. But be sure to shoot with the sun hitting your face and not your back. Or you can purchase an inexpensive lighting kit like on Amazon. Many YouTuber's use these kits to create a great clean look for their videos. Just type in "lighting kit for videos" in your YouTube search bar for great suggestions. Also if your apartment or shooting location has a nice, simple, clean or well decorated area to use as your background for the scene then you wont need to purchase a backdrop. If you do need to purchase one you can get any color that suits your fancy as long as it's a solid color. I purchased a solid white one at B&H and I use it for errrrrthang!

Sound is super important when it comes to filming but in this case as long as your phone is capable of shooting great, clear video your sound should be fine. Just make sure you're close enough to the phone when shooting in order to be heard clearly. For extra clear reinforcement you can purchase a smartphone microphone or a phone boom. You can also purchase a Lavalier, which is a clip on microphone if you're using a professional camera. Again search on YouTube, amazon and B&H for a great microphone for videos. So, if you have an up to date smartphone you are beyond halfway prepared to shoot your own scene or monologue for your reel.

Choose a scene that showcases your awesome acting ability and product. So if your product is a super awkward, funny off beat guy. I'd choose a scene from a movie or a TV show that has a character similar to that description like Ebon Moss-Bachrach's role in "The Punisher", and make sure that character has enough lines and moments to shine and standout as opposed to the other actor in the scene. So yes, if you're doing a scene you will need someone to read with you. They can either be behind the camera or in the actual scene but either way, you will be directing your attention on the other person and never the camera unless you decide to break the 4th wall (the 4th wall is technically addressing the audience and viewers and looking them in the eyes which is the invisible wall straight ahead of you in theater or in this case the camera). When choosing a scene partner, ask a friend from acting class, a family member, a good friend or your significant other. As long as they can read and they're comfortable with being seen or heard on camera and it works, you should be perfectly fine.

After shooting your scene it's time to edit it. Try to keep your reel as short as possible but there is no hard rule about how long it should be. Your reel should move and not drag on at any point no matter how short or long it is. Just because it's short, doesn't mean it's not dragging. Get to the point with your editing. Only showcase the best parts but make sure it all makes sense. You can use some of the scene or all of it, as long as it moves and the emotion of it holds the audiences attention. Like I always say, do you! Just do your best!

I used to roll my eyes at the thought of editing but I'm telling you, I became a little editing maniac! I love editing and I get super meticulous when I do it now. The great thing about editing yourself is YOU get to choose all of your best moments and clips and don't have to go back and forth with someone else who thinks otherwise. I edit all of my footage using an app called iMovie. I do it right from my phone. You can add text to your videos, photos, and music and speed it up or slow it down. If you don't own an iPhone or apple products to edit your footage on iMovie, search in your app store for an editing app with great reviews. You can also use final cut or any of the industries top editing software if that's your thing. Make sure your reel has your headshot in it along with your name and email but not your phone number. If you have an agent or a manager, then use their contact info including their phone number because they are a business and have experience funneling phone calls and sifting through the bullshit that can possibly come your way and waste your time. It might also be a great idea to have a separate email address specifically for your acting.

Keep in mind that if you learn and get comfortable with shooting your own scene you will be ahead of the game because there will most likely come a day when you have to do a self-tape for an audition. Sometimes auditions can't be held in person for whatever reason and actors are cast straight from a self-tape. I probably do at least 20 self-tape auditions per year.

2) Book a student film

If you book a student film you will not only have the awesome experience of working with trained students in film making who will possibly become the next generation of directors, film makers and producers and casting directors but you will have another credit under your belt and hopefully great footage to use for your reel! Most student films do not pay actors. They offer you footage from the project for your reel in exchange for your talent. This is a great barter system for actors looking for experience and footage in the beginning stages of their career.

You can find student film auditions on actrorsaccess.com, mandy.com or backstage.com. You can also check with the performing arts schools in your area and find out how you can find out about and submit for any upcoming projects they're casting. Just submit for roles that are in alignment with your brand or you can just absolutely see yourself playing, send them your headshot and resume and keep a positive mindset about receiving an audition opportunity and hopefully book it! I've done a few student film projects with NYU, Columbia & SVA. I learned so much and created friendships with super talented folks. I also got some great footage from those projects when I was first starting out.

Remember, ALWAYS ask for your footage and stay on top of anyone from production that promises you footage for your reel. This is their form of payment to you and they either gave you their word or put it in a contract in exchange for your talent. Therefore they owe you that footage. Sometimes certain productions are unorganized and not motivated to edit and complete the project for many different reasons and it can be very difficult to get footage in this case. Sometimes the project never gets edited and it's impossible to get your footage. In this case you can either ask them to send you some or all of your individual scenes and if the person is super cool and understanding they might give it to you. But if the project is complete and you haven't gotten your footage, stay on top of them and be relentless! Get your talents worth. You are worthy of that footage and need it. This is less likely to happen if you submit for student films from reputable universities and schools with top of the line film production programs.

3) Pay for someone to shoot and edit your scene or monologue and create your reel.

This is one of the easiest ways to get a reel. If you shoot your own scene(s) or monologue(s) and have footage from a student film or other projects your have worked on and don't want to edit it and create your own reel, you can easily send the video files to an editor and have them put it all together for you for a price. This price can vary depending upon what the editor charges.

It's also super easy if all you have to do is choose a scene(s) or monologue(s) and have someone or a small team do all of the filming, lighting, sound and editing for you. All you might have to do is bring another actor friend with you to read off camera or be in the scene with you. You can shoot this inside or outside, whatever floats your boat. But the best part is all you have to do is show up and act and after you shoot, you're done! The person or small team you hired takes care of all of the technical shit you don't want or care to do. To hire a small production crew or a one person Production Company can cost a pretty penny but it might be worth it depending on your personal needs and available time. Also if you have a friend or know someone who's in film school who's into building their resume and experience they might not charge you much at all. Just decide what's best for you and what resources you may have in order to this for little to no money. Just be sure to ask yourself, "Do I have the time to study lines, break down a script, create characters, learn how to film myself properly, edit my reel and upload it?" Few people don't. I know a few people who do and did it and it came out amazing! But if you are a person who doesn't have that type of time, or not really interested in doing all of that, here are a few options for you..

I have only used 1 of the services I have listed below. Wagthatreel was super professional and fast! They are a full-blown production company and had a great experience with them. They only edited the footage I sent them but they are able to do everything. But after doing a little research, I found a few more companies for you that I listed to make your search and hustle easier. Remember-always do your own research before you spend your money and ask the necessary questions to ensure you can get what you want!

Here's a few Reel Production Companies. For more resources visit Theactorshustle.com

NY

1) https://www.showreelsnyc.com/

2) Wagthatreel.com (I have used This Company and was very happy with my results)

LA

1) www.Lareels.com

ATL

1)http://atlantaactordemoreel.com/

"Hustle beats talent, when talent doesn't hustle." – **Ross Simmonds**

Another great hustle tool every actor should have is..

SOCIAL MEDIA

I used to hate social media but now I LOVE IT! Social media is such a great way to promote yourself for free. And an actor can use all of the promotion they can get.

Social Media really helps actors showcase who they are as a product as well as who they are around friends and family. I think it's good to show both sides. The industry professionals like producers, casting directors, show runners, directors and writers will most likely check to see if you have a Facebook or an Instagram page and when they do, they want to see what you are all about professionally like what your talking about in your posts, how that ties in with your product, what you look like, how many different awesome photos you have, what your lifestyle is like and how many friends and followers do you have that might help them promote their film or show.

My rule of thumb is to just be you and you will shine. Your product and brand is YOU, the part of you that is undeniable and isn't forced. It's just there. It's just in you. So remember to own it and allow it to shine through on your social media. Remember, people follow people on social media because they either know them, want to know them or want to see what this person is doing. This is why it's sooo important to allow your product and Personality to stand out because it's your unique design that was gifted to you and the world will want to either know you or watch you. Embrace that.

What your actor's social media page needs

*A great photo of yourself or your headshot as the profile pic.

*Your short bio should be on every social media page you have. For example:

Shana Solomon
Actor
'Simone Tate' on STARZ's "POWER", 'Karen' on NBC's "Shades of Blue"
I create my own destiny and I love what I do.

Or if I don't have any known TV or Film credits yet..

Shana Solomon
Actor
Studying at PACE University
Lover of the theater & Living boldly
Check out my website below

Keep it simple, use emojis if you want and make it your own.

Keep all pages uniformed. Use the same photo and try to use the same handle for all of your different social media platforms. That way people can easily find you without doing too much.

Add your website link, IMDB link and Link to your reel underneath your bio on your profile pages if they can all fit. You should always include a link to the work you've done to show your page visitors what you're all about. You want them to know you take acting seriously and you're proud of what you do. This can help you gain followers and book jobs.

If you have representation or when you do get representation, you can also put their information as well but that's optional. I put my agents info at the end of my reel, as the main contact on my website and on my resume.

What should I post and how often?

Posting once per day or every other day is ideal but I know that can be a lot for some people especially when you don't have a lot of content. But, with the Internet having so much content readily available to you, you can have enough content to post 3 times a day! It's all depending upon what your product/personality is, what your lifestyle consists of and what vibe you want to give on your social media. Here are some ideas:

1. Quotes (from successful entrepreneurs, actors, athletes, scientists, writers) if it's not your own, just be sure to include the name of the person who created the quote. Quotes are always good for motivational Mondays. You can also post a photo of yourself and include a cool quote in the caption.

2. Meme's. We all love funny and crazy memes. If this is not the type of content you want on your page because of how it looks aesthetically you can always post it on your story and stay in the game of a post per day!

3. Headshots & professional photos. Always post these bad boys! People love a great photo. Be sure to ask your photographer to give you as many photos as possible. Some photographers only give you the edited photos they took of you because they are super particular about how their work is being viewed and represented but if you get a friend to take some shots of you they will usually give you all of them. Now you have some content in the bag.

4. Cool selfies. These work when you actually capture a great shot of yourself or your background tells a story. Like if you're on set, in a cool environment like an all pink restaurant or a baseball game with a huge live crowd or a concert. It also helps when you add a good caption stating what your doing or a quote that hits home for you or your followers.

5. Moments from your acting work. People love to see what you're doing and have done. Like clips from your reel or rehearsals if allowed. Feel free to post your old self-tapes too

6. Videos of your favorite scenes in movies. Especially ones that are in alignment with your product. Like my friend always

books the Italian gangster so he always posts great scenes from the classic Italian mobster films.

7. Pictures of things you like, love or are obsessed with (Coffee mugs, flowers, animals, pineapples, cars, homes, beaches, shoes, boxing matches, famous people) literally anything that floats your boat and gives off great vibes and lets people in on who you are and what you like.

8. Videos of yourself. Shoot yourself on set behind the scenes. People love that! Let people into your acting world. Our world is honestly fascinating and very few people actually have the will power to do it so show the world how strong and amazing you are for being apart of a world that requires so much dedication, intelligence and persistence! Shoot yourself doing cool and interesting or funny things or shoot your cat or dog doing funny things. You can also record how you feel about something that you want to talk about. Just be mindful of the content you're putting out there and always try to be positive.

9. What else do you do besides acting? Do you have a cool ass job that you're proud of? Do you have a hobby like MMA, Makeup, do you shoot pool, tell jokes, are you a contactor or a real estate agent? Take photos or videos of you doing that cool thing and post it! And post others doing it as well. This will only add to your product and give you more depth.

10. Repost other cool content you see on social media that ties in with who you are. Just be sure to give the person you got the content from credit.

11. Post your accomplishments! When you book a role, let your world know if you want to and it's okay with production. If deadline posts about it even better! Just repost that bad-boy and let the likes and comments roll in! Some actors also post there before or after photos of when they audition. I personally

don't do it because I'm usually in focus mode before and afterwards I'm usually focused on getting home or going to get something to eat. But do what floats your boat.

12. Tent-pole. Tent-poling is where you take advantage of a holiday or a big event that is happening and find or create content to post that highlights it in order to create more engagement with your audience. There's always a holiday or a big event coming up. Weather it's a new movie, Christmas, mother's day, SXSW, Coachella, national dog day, national women's day or summertime. You can post about them all by using someone else's content and giving them credit or creating your own using an app like CANVA or OVER. I use both to create all of my original posts, quotes and to tent-pole on social media.

The number one thing to remember about posting is to stay consistent. Weather you do once per day or once per week, make sure you stick to it. Your viewers other than your friends and family are following you because of your content, so keep them engaged.

If you would like to post more often but don't have the time, you can use apps like Hootsuite or Planoly to help you schedule, manage and organize your posts. Hootsuite and planoly can manage multiple social networks and allows you to schedule all of your posts ahead of time. It will automatically post for you once you input what you want to post. I absolutely love Planoly.

Also follow other actors, writers, casting directors, directors, producers and projects that inspire you. You want your timeline to be filled with inspiration and information that can keep you on your toes and let you know what's happening in your industry. Feel free to comment on their pages when you are really moved to do so but don't be creepy.

So hopefully if you aren't already addicted, I hope you end up appreciating social media like I reluctantly did. It can connect you to the acting world, help you book, promote your brand and grow a following to use as leverage in casting and with brands to put more money in your pocket.

"Live daringly, boldly, fearlessly. Taste the relish to be found in competition – in having put forth the best within you." – Henry J. Kaiser

WEBSITE

Does an actor need a website? Yes.

I know I'm repeating myself but I don't care. You are a product. Every product needs to be advertised and have it's own website.

Isn't social media enough advertisement for my product? NO!

You can never have enough advertisement for YOU. Also what if Instagram or Facebook or twitter had some glitch and completely shut down? What happens to your product? How will you connect with people now?

> *"Always put yourself in the position to be in charge of your own destiny." -* **Shana Solomon**

Your website is where everyone gets to really check out your work and product.

Here's what you should have on your website.

*A Bio. A good bio goes a long way. You can write in the third person with some personality similar to this bio:

Shana Solomon, is a writer, producer and an award winning character actor known for her TV roles on "Law & Order SVU", HBO's "Divorce", Starring Sarah Jessica Parker, "The Deuce" starring James Franco and her recurring role as Karen on NBC's "Shades Of Blue" Starring Jennifer Lopez and Ray Liotta. Shana's newest TV roles will be on STARZ' hit drama, "POWER", NBC's New Amsterdam and BET's "First Wives Club" with Jill Scott.

Solomon has also starred in films that were big hits at the 2017 Sundance film Festival, "The Big Sick", a comedy starring Ray Romano and Kumail Nanjiani and "Crown Heights" with Keith Stanfield.

Recently Solomon's one-woman web series won 3 awards at New York City's Hip Hop Film Festival including best actress and best web series for, "The Closet B.I.T.C.H", a dark comedy where Shana plays 11 characters about a woman who falls apart while trying to make everyone else happy. Shana co-wrote and co-produced the series with director and editor William Alexander Runnels who also received an award for best editor and nominated for best director. The Closet B.I.T.C.H was adapted from the one-woman stage play where Solomon performs 19 characters and Runnels also directs. The Closet B.I.T.C.H series can currently be seen on YouTube for a limited time.

Example of one of my first Bio's, it was kind of dry but it was what it was.

Shana A. Solomon—always watched movies and plays, repeating the words, facial expressions and emotions that emanate from characters—always an actor. She attended the Deena Levy Theater Studio, New York. Shana has acted in independent films, television, theater and commercials. Her career has included playing a wide variety of character types and is also currently writing stage plays and screen plays to give herself more opportunity in the arts.

Or you can just keep it genuine and super personal by making it sound like YOU. Check out a really cool example of that here:

EXAMPLE:

What's up guys! I'm Shana Solomon, I'm from the Bronx, New York and I'm an NYC actor who's currently studying the Meisner technique at the Deena Levy Theater Studio as well sharpening my craft of learning how to make you laugh and coming up with witty, snappy comebacks by studying improv over at UCB. I've been in some major one-acts in my scene study class that would've gotten me a few TONY awards because I slayed every performance but unfortunately the TONY nomination board couldn't make it. The only people who were able to make the performances was everyone's mom, dad and best friend who showed tons of support and I was super grateful for it!

I've been in some cool student films such as "The baby shower" directed by NYU student "Jessica Sampson" and "First Dates" Written by Columbia student, "Talibah Newman". My next project is this awesome hilarious play called "Staright Drama" written and directed by "Melonie Miller". Opening night is Feb, 2nd at 8pm. Get your tickets now and see how funny everyone is by clicking this link "inset Link".

*Remember, It's YOUR website so stick to the facts when it comes to your experience and work and if you can, make it funny or personable but always make your website and bio reflect you and your brand. It doesn't matter how long or short your bio is but I always believe it's best to keep it simple.

You should also include on your website..

1. An Embedded Reel. You can use the YouTube player. If you are worried about privacy then just make your video unlisted on YouTube so that only people who visit your site watch your reel.

2. Photos-Promotional/Headshots/Lifestyle & behind the scenes. Put more than just your headshots up there! People want to see who you are and what you do. Take some lifestyle shots of you walking around in San Diego, in a thrift shop in the East Village or having a salad at an outside restaurant in ATL. Put the photo of you in the cast chair or the still of you caught while acting in a scene or at the wrap party. Let us all into your amazing world. (Also use these ideas for your social media)

3. Social Media Links or Embed your twitter or Instagram feed into your website. This is an easy way to gain more followers and more fans because people can see how active and interesting you are on your social media.

4. A blog or updates on your career. Don't write in the third person. Here is where your personality really gets to shine through and connect with people. We need more of that in this world. For example, "What's up y'all? I'm super excited that the film I shot last summer just got accepted into the SUNDANCE FILM FESTIVAL! WHOO HOOOOOOOOOOOOOO! I think I'mma buy myself a glass of champagne tonight!" It's so much more refreshing and it makes people want to actually support you and be a fan.

5. A business email or your manager or agents contact info. Whichever you prefer or have. Some actors just don't want to be bothered with the bullshitters and phony folks in the industry and rather put their agents and managers info on their site to avoid any awkward confrontation and drawn out

conversations about working on projects that will never happen. This can start to happen as your career progresses and you get to a level where a lot of people are trying to get at you and use you. I have my agents info on my website and when I didn't have any representation I used an acting email address I created tat was separate from my personal one. Also, I think it's always great to collect the emails of those who are interested in what you do enough to give you their contact information. If you ever decide to produce your own one-man or one-woman show, theater production, film or web-series and want to let people know about it and sell tickets, you've already got some emails that can help you with that. You might want to raise money and do some crowd funding for a film your in or producing and these contacts are from people who already believe in you so why not start with them? I also have an email grabber so I can collect emails from fans and people who want to receive updates on my career and one-woman show. Some people like to call it a subscribe button. Have your web designer or teach yourself how to install one on your site.

6. A website you can update. This is super necessary as you are going to have new photos, bookings, experiences and growth as time goes on and your website should stay relevant. You want a website that's super easy to update on your own or hire someone who can do it for you. I have used WIX.com and it was super easy to update my website at anytime. There's a monthly fee for wix if you want to use your own domain name. I think it's totally worth it. Some people love squarespace.com. They have really lovely templates but I've never used their services. I now use FIVERR and hire someone to update it when necessary because I want a website that is more tailored to my needs.

"All good actors are smart. We have to read multiple scripts, research characters, words and worlds we've never been introduced to in order to understand how to tell a story that makes sense. We do so much internal work and so much thinking that most never realize. I give credit to actors because our minds are always learning and stretching." **–Shana Solomon**

Another hustler's tool is..

A PRINTER OR PRINTSHOP NEAR YOU

Every actor needs to be able to print out their sides for auditions, table reads (they usually have a copy of the script already printed out when you arrive so be sure to ask ahead of time for table reads), scripts, plays and contracts and sometimes you have to print these out on the fly. My agent has sent me auditions 3 hours before my audition time. Luckily I have my own printer and can make quick moves like that. This is why it's best to have your own printer with enough paper and ink to last you a few months.

What are sides?

"When you book an audition, you may hear a lot about "sides."

Sides are a portion of a script. The word "sides" has been an entertainment industry term dating back to Shakespeare's time. Rather than give the entire script to every actor in a play, actors got only the lines and cues for their specific roles. This helped them save on paper, and prevented rival theater companies from stealing each other's scripts.

These days, "sides" mean the part of a script provided to actors for use in an audition. Typically, sides are available in advance of the audition. How much in advance depends on the project. Just as Shakespeare and his competitors guarded their full scripts, today commercial, film and television productions still use sides for auditions to reduce costs and prevent scripts from being leaked to the internet, or ruined by spoilers, or stolen outright.

What is a table read or a reading?

The read-through, or Table Read, is one of the most important stages for film and theatre production. It is when an organized reading of the theater, film or series script is conducted around a table with a narrator and actors. The Table Read for a green-lit production usually takes place towards the end of pre-production, before the first shoot date, and before any rehearsal period. It gathers many of the cast members and production team together to read through the script and hear the story come alive for the first time.

I have been to many table reads and some of which I was hired to only fill-in for the reading and other times I actually booked the role of the character I read for. You never know how or when an opportunity may knock on your door so take every positive opportunity that comes your way. Just be sure to turn off your phone during a table read. I had theee most embarrassing experience during my POWER table ready where my loud ass annoying ring tone went off when my fiancé called. And of course I tried to hit that side button to silence it but ironically couldn't find it fast enough. Saw a few eye-rolls but everyone eventually got passed it. I on the other hand felt like the only asshole. So show up on time, which means 10 minutes early, pre-read the script if you can and try to work on your character as much as possible to find the funny and powerful moments so you can shine at that table read!

"Audiences are harder to please if you're just giving them effects, but they're easy to please if it's a good story." – **Steven Spielberg**

My approach to acting is simple, either I read the script and I get it or I read it and I don't. If I don't get it, I can't do it." -**Shana Solomon**

THE IN'S

The "In's" are any website, publication, event, group or class that gives you info on upcoming auditions, meet and greets or a way to connect with casting directors, directors and producers that would be interested in you for current castings. Like actorsaccess.com.

About 10 years ago I got really fed up with not knowing what's going on in my industry. I didn't know how to get an agent, even though I read books on how to get an agent or a manager but the advice didn't work for me. I didn't know how to get an audition on my favorite shows or any series for that matter or any kind of respectable film because I thought I needed an agent or a manager and I didn't have that. I had no idea where to start even helping myself. I was pulling my hair out and honestly an emotional wreck because I didn't know what to do and was spinning in circles. I thought I did everything right because I did exactly what I read all actors should do and have in order to become successful. I went to acting school and got my certificate, I took improve courses, I had my headshot and resume, some student film experience on my reel, I had my 2 monologues ready to go, my website was on point. For 2 years I took one on one Casting director and agent classes to perform for them and meet with them in hopes of them seeing my talent and want to cast me or add me to their roster, I mean I had my shit together. I even had my mother help me mail out 25 comp cards per week to casting directors, agents and managers I found on IMDBPro.

By the way, Comp Cards are post card size cards with a few different headshots showing different looks with your information, website and what you've recently booked all on the card. I did that for a whole year but nobody ever responded. I was about to fucking quit. Until I stopped into the Drama Book Shop in NYC on west 40th street to see if there was any info on auditions that I missed other than backstage. At the time, backstage was only giving me certain theater, and indie or student film auditions) and the guy at the front told me about these lists.

The first List was a list of all of the Network TV shows and films being shot in NYC and the casting directors for each project was also listed but there was no contact information for the casting director.

The second list was a list of all of the agents, managers and CASTING DIRECTORS in NYC with their office location, email and phone numbers. Jesus take the wheel! I threw about 7 parties; bungee jumped, did a dance performance and screamed at the top of my lungs all in my head when he showed me that second list!

With the information from these two lists, I realized I had all I needed to succeed. I had the key to the hustle.

See, meeting with and performing for casting directors is one thing. But meeting with casting directors who are currently casting for shows that I can actually see myself on and know I would be perfect for is another.

My old Method:

"Let me look on actorsconnection.com or oneonone.com and see which casting directors are having an upcoming class" Pay anywhere from $40-$350 for the class with a casting director who might be on a casting hiatus or not casting anything that I or they can actually see me playing a role in. Whelp! My photo gets added to a pile and I drift into the abyss of actors who he or she doesn't need right now and possibly get forgotten about unless I slayed my scene in the most memorable way and even then if there's no project that I'm perfect for right now, nothing really happens other than an awesome email from the casting director about keeping me posted. Which is a great thing because a relationship is being built but we as actors want more. We want action and movement and to get the ball rolling on getting in that audition room for that project that's being cast.

My new method:

I know exactly what's being currently and soon to be casted and shot in my area. I also know who's casting each project. Let me make a list of all of the projects I would be perfect for and I can see myself getting cast in because I know my product. Now that I have my list of productions along with the casting director for each one, let me look on actorsconnection.com, oneonone.com or standupshowcase.com and see which casting directors who are currently casting my "Product" and are having an upcoming class". I'll Pay anywhere from $40-$350 for the class but will attend each class prepared and with the intention of showing them my product. If I kill my scene or monologue, or perhaps they see something special in my product, I have more of a chance of getting called in for an audition right away or sooner than later.

See the difference? One is running off hope and drive and that's cute and all but there's no clear system with steps in place to reach your goal. So you'll just be dilly-dallying forever until someone thinks you're worthy enough for a shot.

Fuck that! You don't have time to wait until you are chosen. You must decide you are already chosen and show them what they have been looking for and need at the perfect time! You need a system.

THE DEFINITION OF **SYSTEM**

A set of principles or procedures according to which something is done; an organized scheme or method.

Having a system gives you clear vision, understanding and most of all, intention.

There's something really powerful about INTENTION. It shifts you from being hopeful with your hand out to being unstoppable and respected if used correctly.

THE DEFINITION OF **INTENTION**

A thing intended; an aim or plan.

Writing this is getting me crazy hyped! This is reminding me when I changed the game for myself. I remember I turned into a beast! A hustling actor beast. I just want the same for you. I want you to do everything in your power with respect to your morals and others, to obtain every goal you have, especially when it comes to acting because people make it seem like there's some kind of invisible barrier and it's true! Theirs is but it's not what you think. The barrier is to keep out the weak. And you my love are not that. If passion burns inside of you to make it in this business, then you have the foundation of a strong actor who will make it. You just need the tools and knowledge to succeed.

So I have good news and I have bad news and lets just get the bad news out of the way.

The Lists the man gave me in the front of the Drama Book shop no longer exist and the Drama book shop is currently closed because Lin Manuel Miranda, creator and star of the hit Broadway play Hamilton, purchased the drama book shop in order to save it from going under. Which I'm so thrilled about because that place quickly became my sanctuary and daily go to spot to read plays and books on the business for free because I had no money. I've read in a few articles that it should be opening sometime soon.

But I compiled a list of websites where you can find the exact same info for NYC, LA, GA and all other current film locations. Make a list of the productions, TV shows, Series, films) in your area that you think your product would fit perfectly on. Weather the casting directors name is attached or not is totally fine and you'll see why below.

MY LIST OF "In's"

Filming in NYC NOW

http://www.projectcasting.com/news/filming-in-new-york-city/

https://www1.nyc.gov/site/mome/industries/filming-now-in-nyc.page

FILMING IN GEORGIA NOW

http://www.projectcasting.com/news/now-filming-in-georgia/

https://www.ajc.com/blog/radiotvtalk/what-shows-are-production-atlanta/6x3OggbGqCT6VI37QTZTeI/

FILMING IN LA

https://onlocationvacations.com/

FILMING EVERYWHERE Cost: $139 per month

This industry website and newspaper hands down gives you the most up to date, spot on information. If you subscribe to variety, you will get loads of necessary info including a production chart. Production Charts list every pre-production and production commitment across TV and film for all projects with expected distribution in the US.

So if you live in New Orleans or Florida, you will have full access to what's being casted and shot in your area. You will need to know what's being shot in your area in order to really hustle with or without an agent. You should always know what's going on.

https://variety.com/subscribe-us/

Now you need a list of all of the casting directors and their contact info that are casting the projects you've listed. This can be found on a few free sites like https://castingdirectorslist.com/, which is free, or sign up for an IMDbPro account. Which has an annual subscription but is usually up to date and on point. Search for the casting directors name and then open their contact information page. IMDbPro is an information gem. I have had an IMDbPro page for almost 10 years and it has been such a big help finding contact information for just about any casting director, agent or manager.

HERE'S THE HUSTLE

Once you know which casting director is casting the project you want to audition for you should do these 2 things.

13. Look for that casting director on actorsconnection.com, oneononenyc/la.com, theactorsgreenroom.com, oneononenyc.com, standupshowcase, or any organization that offers classes and meet and greets with casting directors.

14. Take their class or course, prepare your scene or monologue and also have a few questions handy pertaining to the project they are currently casting. It's always great to ask questions because it makes you more memorable and also helps you understand anything you don't know and need or want to know Most people are too shy to stand out by asking questions but this can be important especially if it's a great question.

You can ask questions like..

> *"Are you currently casting for roles for (TV show or Film they are or will be casting on your list)?"*

> *"If an actor doesn't have an agent, how can they submit themselves for (TV show or Film they are or will be casting on your list)?"*

> *"Who are some of the agencies you respect and work with that send great talented actors your way for auditions?"* or *"What are some really great talent agencies out there that I should align myself with?"*

> *"What are some of your pet peeves that an actor does in an audition?"*

> *"What are the main things an actor should do or be aware of to ace their audition?"*

> *"Can non-union actors who don't have an agent submit and be considered for a role on (TV show or Film they are or will be casting on your list) and should they be prepared to pay for their sag card immediately?"*

> *"What made you become a casting director?"*

> *"What do you wish you would see more of in the auditioning room?"*

> *"What books do you recommend for actors to read?"*

> *"Do you have any advice on how an actor should handle not booking the role especially when they know they did amazing?"*

These questions will set you up to prepare and win. They give you the necessary information to take specific action and hustle to get into the audition room and book the role!

Not every casting director will give you the answers you're looking for or think your looking for but trust me, some most definitely will. Remember, every piece of information you get leads to a better stronger you. It's up to you to throw away the unnecessary and negative information and keep the positive.

If someone tells you that you need an agent to submit, take note of it and continue to meet with other casting directors who don't require an agent's submission. Some casting directors like to solely work with actors who are represented by agents because it gives them the comfort and the belief that an actor will be prepared, is professional or must have something special since they are being represented by a specific agency. Which is totally understandable. But some casting directors just want the best actor for the job and can tell that you are professional and have something special on their own and don't need anyone else's stamp of approval. They are out there and if you hustle and continue to push you will find them. A lot of actors get called in at meet and greets with casting directors. I have personally been called in a few times.

After you crush your scene or monologue or one on one with the casting director of your choice, and you know you and that casting director had good vibes after your performance and after your questions, they might call you in to audition for the project on your list. But regardless of what happens, send them an email the following business day letting them know that it was a pleasure meeting them, thank them for their time and information and you look forward to working on projects with them in the future and to please keep you posted on projects you would be great for. Keep it simple but keep it YOU. If they didn't offer you their email, don't go looking for it in order to email them. You will see them again if you continue your acting journey and every time you do, you are strengthening your business relationship with them.

The goal here is to audition and book work but also create relationships!! Relationships build the foundation to an actor's hustle and ultimately their success.

I met a casting director at actorsconnection.com and got called in within a few days for a Broadway play called "Stickfly" produced by Alicia Keys. I didn't book it but I did great on my audition and that initial meeting sparked the beginning of a healthy actor/casting director relationship. This casting director consistently called me into her office and shared the office with other popular casting directors and by the other CD's seeing me coming in and out of the office helped me to build a rapport with every casting director there. I eventually booked a role with a casting director in that office on HBO's "Divorce" a few years later and now they all know me and greet me by my first name and I know theirs. See, I planted that relationship seed years ago, kept it professional and always showed up on time and prepared.

If you do a few of these casting director classes per month with intention, you might just book a role out the gate! Who knows, but you will build a hustle foundation, which will eventually lead to you booking a role. Be patient yet diligent.

Another way to hustle the information of knowing what's being currently filmed and casted in your area and having the casting directors information for each project you might be prefect for is you can just simply email the casting director. MOST INDUSTRY PROFESSIOANLS WILL TELL YOU TO NEVER CALL. And you should be very mindful and respectful of this rule but I also say, If it's a burning desire and you know you would be perfect for this role, ONLY EMAIL IF YOU KNOW THE SPECIFIC ROLE AND PROJECT YOU ARE AUDITIONING FOR AND IF ITS CURRENTLY BEING CAST. If you somehow heard that auditions were being held next week for a specific role and have the breakdown for that role you can give it a shot as long as you are respectful and submit yourself. I believe this no call rule industry standard came from creepy, needy weird actors overstepping their boundaries and making it super uncomfortable for casting directors because these actors didn't know what they were really submitting for. You can't just send an email saying, "Hey Ms. Cohen, I'd love to audition for Law & Order. Here's my headshot and reel. Let me know which role you think I'd be perfect for and I'll come in an audition." Your email just annoyed the shit out of someone. You are supposed to make their jobs easier but this email just made it harder. Do you think they will say to themselves, "hmmm, let me take 20 minutes out of my day and see which roles we're casting for and see where this lady fits in?" Nah. Never gonna happen. I'm sure this rule is also in place because if every actor called or emailed a casting director, they would never get their work done. So leave this hustle route to the last resort and only if your absolutely sure about what role you're submitting for and have the proper information.

Many actors become weird when they are around industry professionals such as agents and casting directors because actors hold them in such high regard that they make themselves feel inferior which can cause them to overcompensate. When a person feels inferior, they have a defeated energy about them and can come off very weird to others. This goes against a hustler's mentality and nobody likes a weirdo actor. So always keep in mind you are here to help them succeed just as much as they are here to help you succeed and hold your head up high every step of the way because you are just as important.

Every one loves an actor who knows exactly what they want, knows what role they are interested in submitting for, prepares for what they want, has a great balance of being professional yet comfortable in their own skin even if they're weird. But be that weird actor because you own your uniqueness full out, not because you don't know what to say or how to be or what you want.

When you email the casting director, if you're blessed enough to find their current email address, you might really be emailing their associate or assistant. A Casting associate or assistant is just as important as the casting director because they work day in and day out with the casting director and trust me, most likely that associate or assistant will be running her or his casting office someday.

When you know exactly which role you want to submit for, give them the name of the role and let them know you'd like to self submit for the role of "_____" in "NAME OF SHOW OR FILM". Ask them what is the best way for you to submit. Never ask if it's okay if you submit or can I submit. This world is for the takers. I'm not saying to be rude and aggressive, I'm saying state what you want with grace. And be assertive. Here's an example of an email (names are changed for privacy purposes) I sent to a casting director whose class I've never taken and got an audition for it.

Submission - Character Actress to play Role of "Tonya & Shauna Keating"

Hello Ms. Smith,

My name is Shana Solomon and I am submitting myself to audition for the upcoming film you're currently casting, "Same Difference", for the roles of 'Tonya & Shauna Keating'.

I am currently a recurring character on "Shades of Blue" on NBC and shooting season 3 until September 15th. I've also had a 3-month off-Broadway run of my one woman show "The Closet Bitch", where I perform 19 characters.

Here's a 2-minute clip of me playing 4 different characters in a short film based on my one-woman show. (Clip)

I have also included my headshot, website and reel for your review.

REEL:
https://vimeo.com/152187867

Website:
http://shanasolomon.com/

Please let me know if you need any further information in order for me to audition. I look forward to working with you and have a great day.

Thank you,

Shana Solomon

    She responded to my email and said she would check my materials. I did not get an audition but at least I got a response. I was respectful, knew exactly what role I was submitting for, and for what project. I sent all of my materials including my reel to make her job easy to determine if I was the right fit for a specific role and I only sent one email. Just because you don't get an audition form sending out 1 CD an email doesn't mean you quit. You keep going and persist until you succeed with other casting directors and opportunities.

    I barely email any casting directors anymore. I do not receive any under the table breakdowns. So, if I don't have the necessary info needed to submit myself, I wont do it. However, if someone I know in production tells me it's okay to email my materials to casting, or if I get notice of a casting in other ways or have a good relationship with the casting director then I will do it. I basically use my gut instincts; respect the casting director's space and how they do business. And I always tell my agent about all auditions and bookings I make on my own. I just like to put everything on the table and make sure we're all on the same page.

    Here is an email I sent to a very well know casting director after taking her class. I took her class years before I sent this email hoping she would remember me. I really wanted to take her class because she has casted some of my favorite films and usually casts "my type" and I thought this would be a great business relationship to start planting seeds on. Her class was absolutely AMAZING and filled with jewels. She responded by asking me to send in a self-tape audition for another role!

Subject line: Your Former Student- Shana Solomon's "JADA" YouTube Audition

Hey Karen,

Hope all is awesome. I know your getting a ton of submissions and putting out massive fires but when you get the chance i'd love for you to checkout my "Jada" audition link from the current sides for the role.

(Include link)

Thanks for watching!

Shana Solomon

KARENS RESPONSE:

Please retape with the role of Left Eye.

Return to both email addresses above.

Sides attached

Karen Casting

After I sent her exactly what she asked for this was her response..

Thank you Shana!

That response was definitely short and to the point but it was also all I needed to let me know that I made the right move! Did I ever book these roles? No. But I planted more seeds to develop key relationships that will be beneficial to my career growth. Putting yourself out there in a positive way gets you exposure and you almost always get on that CD's radar for future roles. Just think, if your audition rocked, and got a response, you might just book the next audition with that same CD. I continued to email CD's when I felt it was a good fit and I started to develop a professional way about myself and it boosted my hustle confidence. Everything I did, every action I took has everything to do with where I am now. And just because I didn't book some of these jobs, doesn't mean you won't book. Everybody has his or her own path. Your path might lead to booking the first role you email a casting director about. But always remember work begets work. Every action leads to a reaction so make sure your actions are wise. When you make moves like this with good intentions and a plan, it will lead to other open doors. You might not be able to see those doors initially but they will appear and open and you will be prepared to walk right on through. So stay on the path.

> *"I excel because of my non-stop, work ethic. I'm always writing, rehearsing, doing readings, podcasts, creating my own work, auditioning, working with other people on their work, networking, reading books, scripts and acting. I hustle my ass off to achieve what I want."* **-Shana A Solomon**

> *"Acting is a lot of work but I absolutely love it, it's so much fun! It never feels like work to me."* **Shana A Solomon**

How do I know exactly what roles are being cast for current projects???

This information is called a breakdown.

A breakdown is a write-up of a project that includes the synopsis, roles and characters needing to be cast, the type of project, the sides for each character, sometimes a full script, producers, directors, writers and casting directors involved in the project and more. This usually gives the actor all the necessary info they need in order to audition.

A breakdown is what gets submitted by casting directors or anyone affiliated with a project when that project is ready to be released to talent agents and managers and sometimes the acting community. Agents and managers then submit the info of the actors on their roster they think should be considered for the role to the casting director. The casting director then lets the agent or manager know that they would like to schedule an audition for that particular actor. That's when the agent or manager sends out and email to the actor for their upcoming audition. The actor responds to the agent or manager stating weather or not they are confirmed or not for that particular role.

This is just about every actor's initial goal, to have a great agent or manager to do the work for him or her. Yes it makes life easier but what if you also learned to do it for yourself? If you did, you will most likely naturally attract an agent because you are already building relationships with casting directors they work with and will be submitting you to which makes their jobs easier. Also even when your agent is working to find roles to submit you for, you are doing exactly the same for yourself. Maybe not as much, because I barely do it anymore because luckily my agents keep me busy but I still network my ass off. But If I do self-submit I always communicate with my agents before doing it just in case they already have submitted me for the same project and just haven't heard anything yet. But by doing this you will increase your chances on building more relationships and booking more roles.

These breakdowns are found through a service called Breakdown Express through Breakdown Services. These breakdowns are released only to qualified subscribers.

WHO GETS THESE BREAKDOWNS?

Only licensed talent agents and managers are allowed to subscribe to Breakdown Services for the Theatrical Breakdowns. No one else is allowed to get the breakdowns, and those who receive them through Breakdown Express are not allowed to share them with other people. The projects posted in the Theatrical Breakdowns with Breakdown Services include feature films, TV movies, reality TV, episodics, pilots, short films, industrial films, theatre, a small number of commercials, and some print and modeling projects.

Now some folks get these breakdowns and sell them to actors to hustle their way into the audition room without an agent. I would not advise this. I know I can't stop a hustler, so if it ever comes your way and you must take advantage of this situation, please do so respectfully and wisely and go get what's yours but I do not advocate this.

The Breakdowns that are released to actors can be found on many websites such as

1. Actorsacess.com
2. Backstage.com
3. Broadwayworld.com
4. Actorsconnection.com, oneononenyc.com and the actorsgreenroom.com (will sometimes tell you a CD is currently casting for a particular project. Sometimes CD's like to keep this under wraps.)
5. Mandy.com

6. Join and follow Facebook groups and Instagram accounts that let actors know about upcoming auditions.

These breakdowns are super useful and will help you build as you move up the ladder in this industry. I don't want you to think you can or can't start off with a network TV or studio film role. Again, your path will be unique to you. I know a young actor who did one web series and then booked a guest-starring role on POWER. I used all of these at some point to get to where I am. Use every tool you have within reason to get what you want.

GETTING AN AGENT

What is the purpose of an actor's agent?

An agent's job is to use his or her contacts and inside information to get you acting gigs. This is how it works; the agent submits you and your info (headshot, reel, resume or your most recent work) and sometimes even pitches you and your brand over the phone for an audition with the casting director, producer, director and or executives. If casting is interested they send the agent all the info needed for you to audition. You then receive an email from your agent regarding the same info which is usually the time, place, production information, start date, character breakdown, weather it's film, TV, a series or theater and the audition sides and sometimes the script. Agents have a roster of clients (actors) who they do the exact same thing for. You may at times see someone from your agency auditioning for the exact same role you're auditions for. But don't worry. What is for you is for you. The agents main concern is that they get you in the room to audition with as many CD's and industry professionals as possible to increase your chances of booking work so you can both make money and grow in your careers.

Getting a good agent that's right for you can be difficult but it's not impossible. Like anything, it takes a plan backed with action and persistence. Remember; be open to opportunities that aren't part of your concrete plan. Those are the lovely doors you have attracted to open by taking massive action on your plan of achieving your goals. I will explain what I mean after I give you 3 examples of me hustling for an agent.

Here's some awesome info I got from Monroe Mann, entertainment and criminal defense attorney, that I wished someone had hit me over the head with before I got my first agent..

PRO'S & CON'S OF HAVING AN AGENT

Pros

1. You will have someone or a team of people searching for acting auditions for you on a daily & consistent basis.

2. You will have someone who can negotiate on your behalf from a position of greater power or respect.

3. You will have someone on your team who can support you emotionally as you handle the rejection of this business.

4. You will have someone (it is hoped) to boost your reputation and credibility and pitch you right because typically the more successful actors are the ones with the agents.

5. You will have someone (it is hoped) help you understand to a greater extent, the various entertainment contracts you may be presented with.

Cons

1. You have to give them 10% of your earnings. Be aware of paying out on your residuals! Make sure your contract does not state this. You should never pay an agent or manager residuals.

2. You sometimes have to sign an exclusive contract with them, which prohibits you working on a freelance basis with other agents.

3. Your agent ultimately won't get you any auditions. (IMPORTANT: Your agents job is to get you into audition rooms that you can not get into on your own. Their job is not to ensure you book the role, that's your job!)

4. Your agent may (and this rarely happens) sign you and deliberately not get you any auditions for the simple fact that you are one of this agents other client's competition. So by signing you, they effectively take you off the market.

5. Your agent may interfere with your taking other jobs.

6. Your agent is not an attorney and you need to always be aware of this fact.

*Get an attorney and have a licensed professional read any contract before you sign it. Basically, having an agent just to say, "I have an agent" is a foolish thing to do. That is driven only by your ego. You do not want an agent unless you know for a fact that this agent really likes you and your work, really supports you and is actually going to make sincere efforts to send you out on auditions because they believe in you. If they can not promise you that, WALK. Any agent you work with needs to prove those things to you.

So you want an agent right?

Do you know what agency you would like to be represented by and why?

A lot of actors want to be represented by an agent and could care less who they are, what other actors are on their roster and what their accomplishments are and what casting directors they have relationships with. Some actors just want to be able to say, "My agent" in a sentence. I made this mistake before because I just wanted someone to save me from the hard work of looking for auditions and building relationships so I could just focus on my acting. Ha! I still had to bust my but and find auditions because "My Agent" didn't have the relationships needed for me to get in the room with top casting directors and book quality work and grow as an actor. I was with this agency for a year. At the time, I looked at it as I lost a year. But If I didn't go through that, I wouldn't be as strong as I am today in order to write this book and give you an easier route.

I've been represented by 3 agencies in NYC. My current Agency is bicoastal and is awesome to the moon and back. I genuinely love the team of agents that represents me. I've been with them for years. But before I signed on with them I have to tell you how it all began in bullet points.

THE AGENT HUSTLE

HUSTLE #1 The 30 day Agent

- I needed an agent badly

- Did no research as to which agency I wanted to work with.

- Got a list of Agencies & Talent Managers in NYC with their contact info from the drama bookshop. You can find an extensive list of agencies in NYC & LA here https://www.

nycastings.com/agent-directory/?pg=1 or ATL here http://www.projectcasting.com/tips-and-advice/talent-agencies-atlanta/ A few of my acting buddies are signed with this awesome agency. I have never worked with them therefore please do your research on any and everyone to see if they are a good fit for YOU! http://www.jpervistalent.com/

- My ex-boyfriend, a fellow hustler and entrepreneur told me to take that list and visit every agency in person with my headshot and resume in hand and be ready to perform my monologues at the drop of a dime. He also advised me to set a date as to when I will be signed with an agency. There were almost 200 agencies and managers combined so, I decided 30 days was perfect. Hahahahaaaaaa! Somebody should've slapped me right here!

- Started my daily agency visits of doing at least 5 per day sometimes 7. Most of which asked me to just leave my headshot and resume because they were so busy and couldn't see me. Some didn't even raise their heads to look at me when we spoke and continued to type or do whatever they were doing. Sometimes you run into such lovely people...

- In my 2nd week I Got cursed out by an agent who shall remain nameless. He told me I would never work in this business again. I took him seriously. I was ashamed and embarrassed and probably cried. But I had a pep talk with myself, called him all different types of assholes and shitheads in my mind while riding the train home, talked to my ex and got my ass back out there the following day to visit 7 more agencies.

- It's been almost 21 days. I'm growing super thick skin but also getting really tired of hearing the word "no" and "place your headshot in the bin thanks". Meanwhile, Ex BF is asking me every single day when I get home "How's it going out there bae? Showing them whose boss?" I'd always reply, "Mmm

Hmm" with a very mediocre fake smile as I slowly died a little bit inside.

- It's the 4th week and I'm feeling depressed and defeated. Still visiting my 5-7 agencies a day.

- No luck at all. I'm pissed the fuck off. I'm honestly ready to quit. But I don't. Plus my accountability partner a.k.a. my ex wouldn't let me.

- It's day 29 and I have an attitude. I mean full out Bitch mode. Not sure why but I started to realize I needed to do something different, something ME, something that would cause me to stand out, be seen and heard but also be respected. I didn't know what that was but I knew I had to do something quick. Day 30 was tomorrow and I knew my ex was going to ask me some annoying ass question like who fell in love with my talent and signed me and I didn't want to tell him "no one". I don't think I slept that night.

- Day 30, I woke up with this fire inside me but I was also completely fucking confused as to what to do with it but I kept my word and went back out there to scratch off the last few agents and managers on my list.

- Every agent gave me the boot or the bin dropping line. I had one last agency and I remember I had a nervous breakdown in Starbucks or some deli before I went up to their office. I wiped my tears and said, "Fuck it. Lets just get this last one over with."

- My hair is shot to shit and I'm not smiling. But I'm not frowning either. I'm just present. I knock on the door. They give me the bin dropping line. I drop my headshot in the bin. One of the ladies at the agency gets up to close the door and I stopped her by sticking my foot in between the door. I looked her in the eyes through the crack and said. "I have visited every single agency in this city and nobody has given me the opportunity to hear my monologue. I'm telling you I'm really good. I not only have talent but I have drive. I mean I've been doing this for 30 days straight visiting at least 5 agencies a day. I've heard almost 200 no's and I just want you to listen to my monologue really quickly and give me a fair shot and then decide if you want me on your team please…"

- She laughed at me. Called me adorable and then opened the door. She asked me to come in and told the whole office how much heart I had and what I just said in a nutshell. She never let me do my monologue but was the first one to take my headshot and resume out of the bin. The ladies at the agency told me they would watch my reel and get back to me.

- They got back to me by calling me and telling me how great my reel was and asked me when could I come back into their office to discuss representation. Whoohoo! I wasn't signed on day 30 but about a week later I was.

See what happens when you push through???

***Remember: Actors shouldn't take this route. Almost all agency and industry professional offices have a policy for actors to never show up in person at their offices. So if you decide to take the route of visiting any agents or CD's office, DON'T MAKE IT WEIRD FOR THEM. Just ask if you can Give them your headshot and resume at most or just drop it in the bin if they have one. No awkward small talk. I honestly think that this is a waste of time because my philosophy is to always build a business relationship by making a connection in an environment that is welcoming of that and a comfortable opportunity for both parties where you can show them your work ethic and talent and they can tell you about their work ethic and goals and following up by staying connected. ***

As much as I appreciated and loved those ladies for giving me my start and being the ONLY agency who said YES, I barely went out on any auditions. I think I went on a few initially but then it started to die down tremendously. I thought it was me. I thought I was a terrible at auditioning. So I took more auditioning technique classes and got back in acting class. Still I wasn't being sent out and whenever I was, it wasn't a role that fit my brand. I realized that the next time I look for an agent, I will research that agency and make sure they have actors booking roles on current network, cable and streaming platform TV shows, series and films that my brand would be good for as well due to their relationships.

Time to change agencies.

I signed a contract that stated if after a year things don't work out with the agency, we could part ways. So we did.

HUSTLE #2 The Connected Agent

- I researched every agent in NYC and created a list of 10 agents I wanted to represent me.

- I sent them mailings of my comp card (a postcard size information card with a few of your headshots and your contact information, social media, website and what you do for example: Shana Solomon, Actor, Comedian, Writer) headshot and resume, emailed them my info and when I saw they were having meet and greets or classes at actorsconnection.com or oneononenyc.com I jumped on it and paid for them.

- At every meet and greet or class I took, I would always have questions ready to go to be sure I would be able to grow with this agency. Looking for an agent is similar to dating is the sense of getting to know them and seeing if this is a good fit for you. Remember * You are interviewing them just as much as they are interviewing you and this also goes for your final meeting before signing.

Initial questions should be

1. What are some of the most recent projects your clients have booked?
2. When you're interested in an actor how do you like to start the relationship? Freelance for a while and see how it goes or do you sign immediately?
3. What led you to become an agent or manager and how long have you been in this industry?
4. How do you like to work with your clients? Closely for example if your clients have questions and need advice will you be available? Not like in a needy way but when it's super important and business related. Email, phone calls okay?
5. About how often do you send your clients out and what is dependent upon that?
6. What casting directors do you have really good relationships with?
7. What do you look for in an actor when thinking of signing new actors to your roster?
8. How have you found some of the actors on your roster?
9. Do you think it's wise for an actor to self-submit for roles?

- After meeting with about 4 agents I found my match from an agency meet and greet at actorsconnection.com and was signed!
- This time it was much easier because I was a lot more experienced and organized. I had a clear vision as to how it

would happen. Also my intention was different. I wasn't begging. I had to learn that agents need us just as much as we need them. They don't make money unless we do. I also built many relationships from the auditions I went on with my previous agent and took many casting directors classes over the years which was really starting to work out in my favor. So this agent was clear that he had a talented actor who also knew a little about the business, had relationships with some key CD's and was a hustler. I was with this agent for a few years. But I did go wrong and forgot one super important chess move before signing which caused me to have to find another agent but we'll get to that in my agent hustle number #3.

HUSTLE #3 The Right Agent

- I booked "Law & Order SVU", A few commercials including "GEICO for the Super Bowl", and a few other films and TV shows. I was growing but not as much as I wanted to. My career felt like it was moving at the pace of a sloth on weed. I was going out for a lot of co-star roles and wanted to audition for guest star, recurring, series regular and lead roles in film. I voiced this to them and it never happened. I remember trying to communicate with my agent to let him know what my goals were but I was usually rushed off of the phone. Communication is very important to me. Again, I looked within and got back in acting class and also started to write my one-woman show, "The Closet Bitch" because I love acting, take my craft very seriously and wanted to play the characters that I would love to be casted in on TV and in FILM. I decided to create my own work in the meantime as I also looked for new and better representation.

- My current non-communicative and rushy agent sent me on an audition for the NBC diversity Talent showcase. This showcase chooses 12 actors out of thousands to perform in front of NYC

& LA's top casting directors, agents and managers. It was a comedy based showcase, non paid, had to be available a lot in order to meet with the producers of the show from NBC to go over the details of the show and rehearse with your scene partner and director. So depending upon what kind of job you have, you might have to take some time off or figure out a new work schedule.

- At this point in my career I was no longer working for free. I needed and wanted acting to pay my bills but I decided to audition for the showcase anyway due to the amazing opportunities that would be available to me if I booked it. I decided I would figure out what I needed to cut back on financially and if I booked it I would cut back on my bartending shifts.

- I booked it!

- Showtime came and every actor was great. I made sure I stood out and did my thing and truly left it all on that stage.

- After The show there was an after party meet and greet shindig and I met soooo many agents and managers. They all gave me their cards and I gave them mine. They all approached me with interest open arms and congratulated me. I must say, this night was a great damn night. The NBC showcase is a great way to excel as a working actor. Actually any of the top networks showcases will propel you as an actor. FOX, ABC & CBS all have diversity showcases. Check them out in the links I've provided below. Hopefully they still work.

Showcase links!

https://www.cbscorporation.com/diversity_institute/sketch-comedy-showcase/

https://www.cbspressexpress.com/cbs-entertainment/shows/2019-cbs-diversity-sketch-comedy-showcase/about

Or NBC Diversity showcase

http://www.nbcunitips.com/nbc-scene-showcase/

- So, the next day after the NBC showcase, I got a phone call from a few agencies and managers. I couldn't believe I was the one being contacted. I looked all of them up and not to throw shade but honestly they were all waaaaaay better than my current agent. I mean these agencies and managers where at the top of my list when I was looking for an agent the second time around. So, I decided to set up meetings with everyone. But this time I wanted to not only be sure they had the proper relationships conducive to my goals and growth but that we were on the same page when it came to those two things, that they actually cared about me as a human being, that we communicated well with each other and didn't have any awkward vibes. I also wanted them to know I needed them to work just as hard as I do, because I'm about growth and my money and my reputation. I asked at least 15 questions on the phone call before the actual meeting with my current agent. I might have been a bit too much but guess what? I felt clear. Then when we met, there were no question marks in my head, all I wanted to do was feel their vibe and energy in person. It felt genuine when I met with these amazing folk. So I signed with them and left the agency I was with. Remember this is a business. Always do things the right way but never allow the fear of moving on stop you from your right and need to grow. I have been very happy and grateful to be with my current agency.

When you're meeting with an agent or manager at their office or speaking with them over the phone to determine weather or not you want to sign with them there are some key questions you must ask in order to be super clear on what you'll be getting involved with for the next year or so with them.

Questions to Ask when you set a meeting with a Rep (Agent or Manager)

1. Tell them what your goals are (be super clear about what you want from them). Can you help me grow as an actor and book a Recurring, Guest, pilot or Series regular roles?

2. How many actors have you helped grow from having little to no credits to having a lot or good quality credits and roles and are now series regulars or booked a pilot or are constantly working?

3. What casting offices do you have great relationships with? (Ask yourself, are these CD's in alignment with the CD's you want to see you?)

4. What percentage will you be taking from me? What will the payment structure be? Do you receive the check and then pay me out or vice Versa?

5. Will this be an across the board Representation?

6. How long is the duration of the contract?

7. Do they Take PC from residuals? No BUENO!!

8. What's most important to you about this actor agent relationship?

9. If I'm not booking a lot, or hardly which I don't anticipate but if that does occur, will you still pitch me and submit me?

10. How long have you been with this office?

11. What do you love about what you do?

12. VIBE VIBE VIBE? Ask yourself "what vibes do I get from speaking with this agent?" What is your gut telling you?

I asked my current agent all of these questions and he gladly answered them with all good vibes. I really love my agent as well as all of the agents in that office. They support me in every way and have even attended my one-woman show. It's really wonderful to look up when you're on stage and see your agent genuinely engaged in your performance. That just made my whole damn night!

I never planned on performing at the NBC diversity showcase and I didn't plan on getting an agent this way either but now my experience can inspire you to do the same and also to tell you to stay prepared and walk through every positive open door because you never know...your goals might be on the other side.

So I just basically gave you a few ways to hustle and get an agent. Well, the first route is incredibly difficult, not recommended, super time consuming, annoying for everyone involved especially for the agents you visit. I STRONGLY SUGGEST YOU DO NOT DO IT. I got away with it but that was like 10 years ago. I only told you that story to show you what I've been through. But imagine if every actor who read this book actually visited every agency? That would be ridiculously terrible for both you and me! Also look at the odds here. 1 agent out of almost 200 signed me and that agency didn't even work out. It also put me in the beggar's seat rather than creating a relationship built off of a healthy agent/actor business relationship.

Also, if anyone has ever told you to do a mass mailing of your headshot and resume. DON'T.

STOP DOING THIS

It's a waste of time and money. Never do it. There's no intention behind it and you know I'm all about intention. This business is not about doing anything aimless, it's about preparation, being so valuable that they can't ignore you. Remember, relationships are key. Random emails and mailings aren't forming relationships.

What if a random guy or a girl sent you a text and photo and you don't know this person from shit and asks you on a date? Would you respond and say, "Sure! Pick me up at 7!?" I doubt it. So it's almost the same thing with CD's, agents and managers.

I also asked my current agent how he finds actors and he said,

"Primarily from showcases or shows we catch an actor in, classes/meet and greets, and referrals from casting directors, clients, or anyone else in the industry (acting coaches/teachers, directors, writers, etc., who we might be friendly with)." –I'd like to keep his name private, Talent Agent.

So after I spoke with him I decided to re-cap, add some more info in this book and be super clear on 3 ways of how to hustle to get an agent.

SUPER IMPORTANT! Before you can hustle anything you must be clear on your plan and know what your intention is. Have you created your plan by doing the work I mentioned above? If not that's okay. You can start right now and here's how.

- Who are you targeting? What agents and managers do you want to work with? What agents/agencies do you want to rep you and why?

- The quickest and easiest way to find an agent or manager that might be great for you is by typing any series or film you can see yourself in into the IMDB search bar. Now, if an actor was cast in those productions to play a role that you can see yourself playing or wanted to play regardless if the actor is similar to you or not in race, gender, look, size, it doesn't matter, click on that actors photo and you will be taken to their IMDb profile page. On their page, underneath their profile photo will say "Contact info" Click that and you will be taken to a page that lets you know who represents this actor and most likely the agents and or managers information. (You will need IMDbPro for this information which is about $17-$20 monthly or $163 annually. I think it's a very necessary purchase for this hustle) Click that agent or managers name and see whom else they represent. Start your research on them and put their info in your phone or write it down in case you need to continue this research later and add them to the pile. Again, do not worry about weather or not they rep someone who resembles you. There is enough money and opportunity out here for everyone. So, while the actor who resembles you or has a similar brand that you have, if they are currently working on a project, another project might be casting for that similar brand/product and guess who might be available? That's right, YOU!

- I want you to research and find 10 agencies and or managers that you would like to rep you and I want you to know exactly why. Is it because of the actors they represent and you want to be surrounded by greatness? Wonderful! What else? We didn't come to play; this is going to be work.

- So, How do you find these agents for free? If you can get the name of the agent or manager of the actors you respect or are booking roles you can see yourself playing but don't want to pay for IMDbPro, you may find their contact info here. Not every agent or manager is listed. https://www.nycastings.com/agent-directory/?pg=1

- What do you look for when researching agencies and agents? Visit every agencies website and comb through their talent pool and see what their talent is booking. This gives you an idea of their connections and relationships and what you might possibly be booking and how your career may eventually look.

- I am going to say it one more time, don't worry if they have someone similar to your type on their roster. What's for you is for you. If it's a perfect fit then it is what it is and doors will open for you. Never focus on what someone else is doing vs. what you aren't. Nobody has time for comparison especially when you were made to be different. There is something about you and your brand that is different from anyone else's.

- Research these agencies and agents. Google them, see what's being said about them. If you like what you see and think they can help you grow and you will add value to their careers then write them down. This is how you target!!!!!

Now you're ready to hustle! Here are your hustle options. You can do 1 or do them all! But whatever you do, make sure it works for you.

#1- Performing in A Showcase-How I got my current agent without trying. Here's a list of a few great showcase opportunities.

- Neighborhood Playhouse is an acting program that holds one of the most respected showcases in NY. It's super reputable and its big alumni include actors like Robert Duvall, Christopher Meloni from L&O, and Allison Janney from "I, Tonya". It's a 2-year conservatory. A lot of the industry attends their annual showcase. Almost every drama & performing arts college (Yale, UCLA, Pace University, NYU TISCH, UC San Diego, American Conservatory Theater, DePaul, Julliard) has awesome and respected showcases that are attended by industry professionals. Also, acting schools and studios (Deena Levy Theater Studio, Esper Studios, Ivana Chubbuck Studio, Stella Adler Studio, Howard Fine Acting Studio) have showcases as well. I've listed some of the best schools and studios so be sure to check which ones work best for you by auditing a class and doing your research. Also, have you ever thought about studying abroad in the UK? I hear they have some of the best programs and schools in the world for studying drama and performing arts. I'll list a few I've heard nothing but great things about below.

- Royal Academy Of Dramatic Art (RADA) I hear this is the leading drama school in the UK. They have a pretty great alumni including Ralph Fiennes.

- London Academy Of Dramatic Arts (LAMDA) I've heard this is actually one of the best drama schools in the entire world. That's a damn good reputation!

- Guildhall School - I hear this is a fantastic school and one of the leading g drama schools in London. Some of its graduates include Ewan McGregor and Orlando Bloom.

- UCB & The PITT For Improv has a great following, alumni and are super respected by industry professionals. The shows and showcases that improv and sketch writers perform are usually attended by top CD's, agents, managers and producers. Improv is super huge and improv actors are needed for commercials the time as well as comedic films and series', comedic relief in dramas and sketch shows. SNL tends to be in the house on the regular there!

- NBC, CBS, ABC & FOX Are amazing as I mentioned earlier.

Bring business cards to all of your performances and showcases! Also, discuss with other actors who their reps are and encourage them to invite their reps. This will increase the chances of you being seen by more agents and ultimately getting signed. This is a great way to get referrals from your peers.

#2 MY FAVE! THE MEET & GREET GRIND

- This How I got my 2nd agent but if you do it right, you will have an amazing experience and a great agent!

- I love this hustle because as actors, we have the ability to have more control of getting an agent by putting ourselves in this situation.

- HOW do you do this? – Become a member and create a profile at Actorsconnection.com same w/oneononenyc.com but you need to audition at one on one with a monologue or scene. Call their offices or go online to set up an audition date and time. Once you become a member start looking on their list of meet and greets and classes. Remember you targeted agencies/agents and managers? Take that list and be on the lookout for those agents meet & greets and classes. If the class or meet and greet is sold out, stalk the website until you book that class or meet & Greet!! Go get what's yours! I stalked many classes in my day and always got what I wanted eventually. You will too if you stay consistent and persistent.

- If you are able to perform a scene and bring your own, get a scene that showcases your brand and highlights your talent so you can shine. A reader will usually be there so bring 2 printed copies of your scene.

- Are you clear on your brand? Did you do your brand homework? If not, what does everyone say that your undeniable qualities and characteristics are? If they were casting a movie what role would they cast you to play? Ask them what's your demeanor off the bat as soon as someone meets you what would they say about you? How would they describe you in terms of your look, type and personality? What role in a TV series could they see you playing?

- I want you to kill your scene when you meet with the agent or manager because I want you to increase your chances of signing with them. And also why not always kill it when your act?

- You usually have time for a brief convo after. Prep those questions I mentioned before. Remember you are interviewing them just as much as they are interviewing you and this also goes for your final meeting before signing

- Write down what value you have that will make them interested in representing you. Here are some things to consider that determines your value.

1. What casting Directors you have relationships with and what you have booked and worked on that is worth conversing about.

2. List industry professionals you've worked with. Like top directors, producers and actors.

3. What you will continue to do with or without a rep to grow in your career as a working actor. This will shine a light on your work ethic & hustle.

4. Why you're looking for representation. Maybe so you can grow in your career as well has help others grow along the way.

5. No need to talk to them about your previous rep experience unless you feel comfortable and it adds to your value. For example, you have outgrown your agency and have reached a ceiling. They are sending you out on co-star and under-5 auditions and you have more than enough credits and experience to be sent out for guest star, recurring and series regular roles.

YOU MUST LET THEM KNOW YOU ARE VALUABLE ON ALL LEVELS. THIS IS NOT COCKY. "I'M VALUABLE" shows them you will make them money but go get yours regardless. It lets them know you have the confidence and foundation to "Make It".

- Ask for their contact info to follow up.

- Send an email saying it was a pleasure meeting you and you learned a lot and are appreciative of the time they took to connect with actors.

- If you liked them, say something like, "I would like to set up another meeting or a phone call to discuss representation because I feel we would both benefit from each other in a great way! I have attached my headshot, resume and reel (if you have a reel) for your review. Thank you.

- Be sure to ask them a question in that email! Like, "if so, what day during the week of "Insert Date" Works for you for our next meeting?"

- Or they will contact you first which is checkmate. If you want to see if this will happen give it 2 days to follow up instead.

#3 REFERRALS & RESOURCES

Referrals are an awesome way to get representation because if a trusted source is saying amazing things about you, your talent and what you bring to the table, then half the work is already done for you. The agents or managers mind will be sparked and they will be interested based on the fact that someone they respect, respects you. Respect goes a long way. This business is tiny so keep it professional, treat people with kindness and give every role your all so you move up further and quicker. If you do, People will brag about you!

I took a casting directors class maybe 8-10 years ago. Twice! And when I signed with my current agent they got me tons of auditions with this same casting director. I always went in prepared and pleasant as always. I had to have auditioned for this woman at least 10 times and never booked a thing. But then one day after working on 'Shades of Blue', I auditioned for her again, but this time she had a new casting associate who used to be the casting associate on shades of Blue. And as always I came prepared and was pleasant and respectful. I finally booked with her! It was for POWER. The stars were aligned but I also know that if I had ever been rude or unprepared when I auditioned for 'Shades Of Blue' it would've affected my chances of booking POWER to some degree.

Referrals can come form your teachers, coaches, CD's, directors, writers, actors that you know personally or have worked with, basically everyone you come in contact with can possibly refer you to not only another job but an agent or a manager. Agents and managers keep their eyes and ears to the streets of the industry so don't be surprised who they know.

How do I get a referral? It's really freaking amazing when you don't even have to ask for one and all of a sudden you get a call from a Rep asking you to meet with them. But in case this doesn't happen. ASK EVRYONE! This is all about intention and attracting what you want and close mouths don't get fed so ask. Ask your classmates, actor friends, co-workers on a project, or actors you have some sort of relationship with who knows your work and especially if they've complemented you on your work if they have an agent and who their agent is. If you haven't heard of them, do your research and if you're interested then ask them if they feel comfortable referring you because you're looking for representation.

Dig through your resources and contacts! This is where you look at everyone you know who works in the industry in any way and say to yourself, "do I have a decent relationship with this person? Do they like or praise my work?" If so ask them to refer you. Don't worry if some people say they're not comfortable asking or if some of them refer you but you don't hear from any of the agents, keep asking different people and always follow up and let it go if you never hear from them. Don't pester people but be assertive. Every time you think of a new resource or contact ASK. This is all about planting seeds.

This takes time but it works.

So these are the 3 ways you can hustle to get an agent or manager. I pray you use these hustles consistently and wisely and take massive action in order to attract and create the acting career you want and reap all of the rewards from it and get all you desire.

But whichever route you decide to take from that list I just gave you, do what best suits your needs and lifestyle and hustle that route until you succeed.

AGENTS AND ACTORS ARE BOTH VALUABLE TO EACH OTHER. YOU NEED THEIR CONNECTIONS & THEY NEED YOUR TALENT, BRAND & DRIVE. –Shana Solomon

The absolute best way to get an agent is to stand out in the agents mind so much that they remember you, love your work, respect your work ethic and are clear on what kind of roles you play brilliantly.

Do the same in order to get a manager.

WHAT IS A TALENT MANAGER?

A talent manager is an individual or company who guides and advances the professional career of an artist(s) in the entertainment industry. The Responsibility of the talent manager is to oversee the business affairs of an artist, advise and counsel talent about professional matters, long term and short-term goals, personal decisions, which may affect their career and help the actor grow financially and positively.

A manager can be just as important as an agent but having both an agent and a manager on your team may not be necessary depending on the stage your career is at. Some actors have either an agent or a manager in the beginning stages of their careers. Whatever works for you is what you should go with. There are many managers that have the connections and relationships with casting directors, producers, directors and production companies and can get you into the same rooms and help you forge great relationships as an agent can. So be open to having a manager instead of an agent if that manager will help guide your career and get you great auditions. But be careful having both a manager and an agent too soon.

The actors that have both should either be super booked and busy and have their managers managing their careers and guiding them in the right direction as they soar to the top or their managers are creating new business opportunities and relationships that their agents can't. I've encountered a few actors who have an agent and a manager just to say, "I have an agent and a manager". These are actors at the beginning stages and aren't booking or doing much of anything. Again, don't feed the ego, feed the goal. If you want both, be super sure that both your manager and agent bring something significant and completely different to the table that you need in order to accomplish your goals as a working actor.

I thought I wanted a manager when I first got with my current agent so I gave it a shot. One day, my agent and manager ended up sending me the same audition for the same day. Immediately I realized this wasn't going to work. But it was my fault, I didn't do the proper research on my manager to see what he brought to the table that was necessary and different than what my agent brought. The only thing I had on my mind was that I wanted to be an auditioning and booking machine.

You also have to keep in mind when you have both an agent and a manager that every time you get paid from an acting job, you now have to pay 2 people a minimum of 10% each. Some managers ask for more than 10%. That's a minimum of 20% taken out of your pay.

And yes, depending on the contract you have with your manager you have to pay your manager even when they had absolutely nothing to do with your audition or booking. Meaning they did not set up or arrange your audition in any way but still expect to be paid even if you found and booked the acting job all on your own and will take a minimum of 10% out of your check regardless. So please have an attorney look over all documents before signing and think about what you could be getting yourself into.

Here are a few lists of Talent Managers to research. Remember to take your time and do your research on these agencies and managers as well as interview them while they interview you. Many of them are good and some of them aren't.

*There are also Agencies on these lists

https://www.backstage.com/resources/search/manager/

https://www.entertainmentcareers.net/resources/ca_talent_agencies.asp

http://www.projectcasting.com/tips-and-advice/talent-agencies-atlanta/

In addition to these sites, you can also check the listings on actorsconnection.com , oneononenyc or LA .com or theactorsgreenroom.com for classes and meet and greets with top talent managers in your area.

> *Remember when hustling to get an agent or a manager, be persistent but don't pester them. There's a difference. Respect and understand an agent, managers and a casting Director's personal space. Your goal is to get on their roster not on their nerves. If you need coaching on how to speak with an agent, manager or a casting director, visit my website for tips, classes and one on one coaching calls.

*"Success will come if you stay focused on your goal. Consistency is key. Consistency will get you just about anywhere and anything you want." -**Shana A Solomon***

*"2 huge keys to success are confidence and preparation. When you're prepared and know what you're doing your confidence is high. When your confidence is high, you become unstoppable." -**Shana Solomon***

3

The Struggle

*People ask me, "How long will it take to reach my goal?" I always say, "as long as it takes." -**Shana Solomon***

You can set a goal for yourself for 30 days and reach that goal or not. Does that mean you give up?

ABSOLUTELY NOT!

One of my favorite motivational speakers, Jim Rohn asked the BEST question at one of his speeches, "how long should a baby try learn how to walk? (He pauses to let that question simmer in people's minds) How long would you give your average baby before you say, "hey enough?" (Crowd laughs) Any mother in the world would say your crazy, my baby's gonna keep trying UNTIL!"

You MUST PERSIST UNTIL you SUCCEED!

This is what I constantly told myself and constantly heard from the people in my immediate circle when the struggle got real.

The Struggle

There are sooo many days of struggle as an actor. I think there are just about the same amount of struggle days when it comes to accomplishing any big goal and major career move but the difference with acting is there is no 1 way to becoming a successful working actor, there's basically no road map. You have to hustle because this industry is a numbers game and also a who you know game and sometimes you have to be at the right place at the right time. There are so many variables. So many actors have their own story as to how they "MADE" it. But I'll tell you this, the ones who worked for it, stayed in it regardless of the hard times and got back up every time they got knocked down and kept searching and pushing for the "YES" amongst the hundreds of "NO's" are the best most victorious stories and acting careers. These are the actors that cherish every role they get and continue to win because they continue to work and hustle because they remember how it was when those roles and phone calls weren't coming in.

This is why I have set up the hustle for you in a particular way. I have set up a hustle that will allow you to experience your own magic. My goal is to show you how to maximize your time and meet as many amazing industry professionals as you possibly can. You need to be out there doing all that you can to put yourself in front of other amazing working actors, casting directors, managers, agents, writers, producers, directors and anyone who is connected with where you want to be and can be apart of your growth and help you move up the ladder in your career. But along this magical path it wont always be easy peasy.

While you are on your journey of getting your foot in the door and becoming a working, successful actor and a star, you might have some rough and weary days. But you must stay in it. I'm only telling you this because it's usually apart of the process. I've watched all of my actor friends go through a lot during their hustle period but the ones that stayed it in are now flying high and being rewarded with series regular, recurring, guest starring and leading roles.

There were days when it was super duper dry for me and I didn't get an audition for months! Then I would get auditions but didn't book anything for a year! I would book a TV role but then the buzz and auditions faded and I had to get back to my other reality of bartending at my job and fake smile when people at my job would say, "hey haven't I seen you on TV? Wait a minute! You're on (whatever TV show they saw me on) so, what's next for you. Anything coming up that I can be on the look out for?" That would just crush my entire soul. Because usually my response was, "not yet but I'm sure something will come up soon." And then there would be this awkward moment of nobody knowing what to say and me wiping down their table or asking them would they like anything else. During these struggle periods I would doubt myself, my talent, my self worth, my look and even my creativity. I would ask myself is this acting thing really for me? I was allowing those moments to break me down. I thought it was my hair, my weight, and my technique. I thought I was the problem. I beat myself up until it felt like I was in a deep dark hole and even when I went outside for air or work it felt like I was in a fog. But then I realized that pitying myself and constantly focusing on what I didn't have and what I wasn't booking and feeling stagnant doesn't do anything except make me feel worse. And when you feel bad, that energy spreads out into the universe and pushes the good positive energy away and just attracts even more bad energy. Did you know worrying makes you relive the same negative experience all over again? And I experienced just that. But thanks to my mother, the positive people in my life, some motivational videos on YouTube as well as myself, little by little I stopped having bad thoughts about ME. I stopped asking myself what I was doing wrong and why wasn't I enough to be chosen for a role and started to do what I wanted to do regardless of what a casting director or anyone thought of my look or talent. I started to do things like grow out my natural hair and rock my Afro which helped me embrace the raw beautiful me. I learned to stop covering my face with loads of makeup, which was one of the most scariest but liberating experiences. I embraced my classic pin-up vintage style and owned it. I started to live for ME. This is when I also started to create my own one-woman show. See, after the struggle period or what many actors call a "dry spell" is usually where an actor gets stronger and finds their true self, learn about self, reinvent self and grow. Sometimes when we are at our weakest, darkest moments and the pain becomes so unbearable, it naturally forces you to change because the mind doesn't want to experience this type of pain anymore. It's almost like a switch goes off within us and says, "That's enough! I can't take this Shit anymore!" and we somehow figure out how to dig ourselves out of that dark painful hole in order to survive or some awesome human comes along and helps us get out of it. But this causes us to forever change because we never want to feel that pain again so we end up thinking, being and moving differently. We rise like phoenixes from the ashes. This is how breakthroughs occur and super genius creative things happen. Because we are survivors. There isn't another option other than living. Either we win or we perish. And perishing ain't happening. Never give up because remember, this too shall pass. Regardless of how long it takes, you will come out of the dark storm and light will shine upon you. But if you don't stick around how will you ever experience that beautiful day that you so greatly deserve? This is how some of the most magical scripts are written and powerful TV & movie roles get booked and portrayed. I lost my mother during one of my worst struggles which made it almost unbearable and impossible to find my way back into the light but I ended up booking my first Guest starring role shortly after she passed and when that role called for me to get emotional in a scene, I was able to tap into the pain I experienced due to my mother's passing and I gave that role all I had and every time the director yelled action, I was able to give them a full emotional performance that was real and connected. This scene caused me to become a recurring character and make a whole lotta money. I was never able to emotionally connect to pain or loss so easily and cry on the spot the way I can now. I used to try and cry which was so forced and unnatural. But now I have to try not to cry, which makes it believable. I would do anything to bring my mother back but reality is she's gone. So I use that as a tool when I need to. My struggles made me a better actor and a better businesswoman in this industry. So if ever you hit that "dry spell", don't be afraid, a change will come. You will shed unnecessary layers and pieces of you and grow stronger, wiser and experience so many blessings and breakthroughs that at first might come in the form of loosing, failing miserably and seemingly unbearable pain that makes you feel like you're literally breaking in half. But you must embrace the storms in order to become unbreakable.

Don't wish things were easier, wish you were better. Don't wish for less problems, wish you had more skills. Don't wish for less challenges, wish for more wisdom. The major value in life is not what you get. The major value in life is what you become. Success is not to be pursued; it is to be attracted by the person you become. **–Jim Rohn**

We suffer one of two things. Either the pain of discipline or the pain of regret. You've got to choose discipline, versus regret, because discipline weighs ounces and regret weighs tons. **–Jim Rohn**

The twin killers of success are impatience and greed. **– Jim Rohn**

Only by giving are you able to receive more than you already have. **–Jim Rohn**

If you guys don't know who Jim Rohn is, please research him. He was one of the world's most influential motivational speakers and my favorite person to help me through the darkness besides myself. He's super chill and has such a great vibe that's never too much. He doesn't push, he just sort of eases his way into your subconscious and shifts your way of thinking with some of the wisest cleaver and witty humor I've ever heard.

4

Stay In It

Congratulations! You have hustled your butt off and you now have an agent or a manager or both! Or you have the necessary information to peruse and get them, Whoo hooo! Great work!

Now that you have representation you might feel like, "what do I do now?" Because you're literally waiting for a phone call or email from your agent or manager about your next audition. It could take a day, a few days or a few weeks at time even months to get your first audition from your agent or manager (it really shouldn't take months, if it does you might have the wrong representation). A good agent should send you out rather quickly.

This is why you must continue to hustle. Maintain the regimen you have built for yourself. Continue to do exactly what you were doing before you got representation. It will help you even more now that you have an agent or a manager. If you don't, you might loose the necessary drive that will create more opportunities and miss out on so much. Your work is never done as an actor.

Don't rely solely on others to get you auditions or to keep growing. I actively network, create my own work, get auditions and book union work on my own in addition to the amazing efforts of my agent. Look at it as YOU are a business owner, therefore YOU have to be the most reliable person in your business which requires you to show up early, work harder than everyone else in your organization, network and keep a positive attitude because the "NO's" still come even after success.

Here's what I do to stay positive and motivated..

I always set a new goal after reaching one.

Goals can be big or small and I like to set both. Writing this book was a big goal for me that I completed in 1 day but the idea had been weighing on my mind for years until I finally set a goal and told my boyfriend who's also my accountability partner when I wanted to have this book written in 30 days. He actually forced me to sit down with a pen and a pad in Starbucks and when I say forced I mean bribed me with coffee, hanging out and good convo which led to talking about he book and then he kind of coerced me into taking out my pen and pad and get the writing. But together we talked and created this book chapter by chapter until we were finished. It took just one day to write it all down. Actually 5-6 hours and lots of Almond milk lattes (even though it took months afterwards to edit and get the book to where I wanted it to be). But my goal was to write it in 30 and with discipline it only took 1 day. This goal Kept me busy and helped me to grow and "stay in it" because not am I only almost always doing something that has to with this book but I am able to help other people succeed in life with their acting goals and help shift their minds to a more positive place. This ultimately has lead me to book more work and create multiple streams of income for myself so I'm not just depending on making a living from acting. Acting is my passion and what I was gifted and put here to do to inspire people and live a happy life. But I decided to multiply the gift of acting and become a producer, character creator, writer and author.

I also remember years ago I had a goal to be the best NY monologue actor and compete in the NY monologue slam. The NY monologue slam was a monologue competition where the best of the best actors in NYC performed in front of judges from the entertainment industry for an award, mentorships, auditions and other prizes. Every actor I knew was either talking about it because they wanted to compete or was too scared to compete. This amazing event was produced by filmmaker, actor and author, Attika J Torrence. So, I auditioned for it, rehearsed for weeks, listened to Eminem's "Loose Yourself" on my way to the slam. I was ready to crush these other actors! I didn't do so well in the first round at all. I actually did horrible round 2. I think I saw a judge yawn. But I listened to the judge's constructive criticism, made some unique improv choices and came back strong in round 3 and knocked it out of the park and won! Goals are an amazing thing. They sort of force you to stretch and grow and become a better version of yourself. I usually set goals that scare me in a good way. If I say to myself "wow I would love to do that but how the hell am I actually going to do that?" And then that weird anxious, butterfly in the belly feeling starts to come over me, which is FEAR, I then say to myself "I'm doing it." And don't stop until I accomplish that goal.

An actor can have many goals, just make sure your goals are small as well as big and that when you reach them they bring you to a higher more accomplished place in life and in your career. This keeps you moving forward even during those "dry spells". Accomplishing goals help to boost your confidence and can increase your knowledge, value and network, which eventually increases your net worth.

Here are 20 awesome goal ideas for an actor to set

1. Book a speaking role in a film.
2. Become Sag-AFTRA.
3. Become AEA.
4. Take an acting or improv class.
5. Take a Casting Directors class that is currently casting a show I'd be perfect for.
6. Get new headshots with a great photographer.
7. Create my actors reel.
8. Get an agent.
9. Book a co-star role on TV.
10. Go on 5 Auditions this month.
11. Book a guest star role this year.
12. Book a recurring role this year.
13. Book a series regular role this year.
14. Book a pilot this pilot season.
15. Write my outline out for my film, series, stage play, one-person show idea I have in 2 months.
16. Start my podcast.
17. Get a great manager.
18. Write the script for my film, series or play within a year.
19. Take a writing or sketch writing class.
20. Create an actors meet up group and stick with it.

After setting one of these goals you have to attach a date to it. Once you have a specific date set to reach this goal you must do everything in your power to obtain it and make it happen! So if your goal is to create an actors reel by December 31st, you now know that there are certain action steps you have to take in order to make that happen and have your reel completed by New Years Eve. So it's time to look at what you need to make that happen. Ask yourself a series of questions to determine what your next step is. Do I have any good quality filmed work that I can edit myself or send to an editor to put on my reel? If you do and feel it's strong enough to create a reel with then all you have to do now is find your editor who's great at creating reels. If not then call up theactorsgreenroom. com, film yourself with your phone or camera, have a friend film you or hire a production company to shoot your scene(s) for your reel and edit it or have it edited. Now make sure you send them your headshot and whatever info they need to add onto your reel so agents, casting directors and people who would like to hire you know how to get in contact with you. Make sure the editors or you complete the 1st edit before Christmas so that if you want to make any more changes to the edit, it's not done last minute and you don't miss your deadline of the 31st. You should have your finished edited reel by the 30th so you can be ahead of the game and when you wake up on December 31st you can exhale and bask in your accomplishment that you are in a better position than you were yesterday.

I also stay motivated by listening to, reading and saying..

Affirmations

Everything we say out loud, and to ourselves are affirmations. Weather it's positive or negative. These words seep into our conscious and subconscious minds and cause us to believe, think and act according to what we have said.

I chose to say, listen to and read positive affirmations. It helps me turn any bad, negative situation into a positive one or think more positively about the situation rather than negatively. Having a positive mindset in this business is So important because there are so many "no's" and lows and trials and "dry spells" and negative people who try to bring you down with their negative experiences mostly due to their own short comings. If you aren't able to block that noise out, focus on the positive things that are happening in your life, pick yourself up, do what's necessary to become a better and stronger you by setting more goals and looking at the brighter side of things and understand that YOUR TIME IS COMING, YOUR SEASON IS COMING and all you have to do is just be patient, continue to push and do the work with a smile, then you won't last in this business. If you don't learn how to flip all negativity that comes your way into positivity this business or life in general could break your spirit. I'm only telling you this because I HAVE BEEN THERE. I have also witnessed other actors go through this. That is why it's super important to hang around other actors who are strong and positive so they can rub off on you and help you through the dark times. But you also have to learn how to motivate yourself and this is why affirmations are so important.

    I constantly read/Listen to audio books, watch YouTube videos, put signs on my walls in my house and speak about motivation, success, happiness and all things positive.

25 Great Affirmations for actors:

1. I will persist until I succeed.
2. I am an amazing actor.
3. For every "no" I hear, I know there's a yes on the way for me and it's coming really soon!
4. I am powerful beyond measure and I can achieve anything.
5. I am amazing and beautiful just the way I am.

6. I am grateful to be alive.
7. I'm booking a series regular role this pilot season.
8. I'm unstoppable. Casting Directors love me because I breathe life into my characters, come prepared and make their jobs easier. I am booked and busy!
9. I love myself.
10. Every time I get knocked down I get back up and win!
11. I create my own work and I attract powerful roles that help me grow in my career.
12. I am unique and I own my uniqueness. I love who I am.
13. I attract roles that take my career to the next level.
14. I create my own happiness.
15. My light never dim's when someone else's shines bright.
16. Every audition I have is an opportunity for success.
17. I attract amazing opportunities every time I step on set.
18. I Attract money and my income is getting higher.
19. I am on this journey to live my dream to the fullest.
20. I am currently living my dream.
21. I am confident.
22. I am constantly evolving to become a better me.
23. I am present and grateful for every moment.
24. Great roles are finding me.
25. I attract amazing, powerful and positive experiences. I am glowing and radiating from within.

Search for "motivational" or "inspirational videos" on YouTube. They helped me tremendously.

Here are 8 motivational & self improvement books that I love

1. The Greatest Salesman in The World By, Og Mandino
2. The 4 Agreements By, Don Miguel Ruiz
3. The Mastery Of Self By, Don Miguel Ruiz
4. Think and Grow Rich By, Napoleon Hill
5. How To Win Friends & Influence people By, Dale Carnegie
6. The Art of Happiness By, HH The Dalai Lama
7. As A Man Thinketh By, James Allen
8. You Are A Badass: How to stop doubting your greatness and start living an awesome life. By Jen Sincero

Get into them ASAP guys and watch how you will grow into a better human being as well as a better actor. You should be feeding your mind positivity everyday all day from what you put into it and what comes out of it. It was a little annoying for me at first because all I used to do was use my headphones to listen to music. Preferably Hip Hop, R&B and Reggae which was cool but it was filling my head with a lot of low vibrational thoughts. Now, I mostly listen to audiobooks and motivational videos on YouTube. And of course I still bump my music from time to time but it's honestly not my first choice unless it's positive high vibration music.

CREATE A VISION BOARD

A vision board is a motivational device. It's basically a positivity bulletin board made up of words, pictures and images on it of what you want to accomplish, who you want to become, where you see yourself, and the things you love. Your vision board is supposed to be placed or hung in an area where you can clearly see it to remind you of your goals and dreams on a daily basis. You can cut out and glue or pin these images and pictures from magazines, books, printout's or wherever you find inspiration. The key is to make it your own and tailor it to your personal positive vision you have for your life and hang it up where you can always see it.

I recently looked back at my first vision board I made about 14 years ago when I first started acting and realized I had accomplished every goal that was on that board. A few of my goals on my vision board were 1) Become a SAG actor 2) book a national commercial and 3) Get on 'Law & Order SVU'.

So start creating a vision board to help you stay in it and accomplish your goals. It's a super fun thing to do and makes goal setting easier. If you can, have a vision board party with your actor buddies or closest friends who would be willing to do this along with you and build together.

AUDITION AUDITION AUDITION

Weather you have an agent or not, you should always find ways to audition and be considered for roles on your own by networking with casting directors, writers, directors, seasoned working actors, producers and show runners, taking any one of their classes as well as subscribe and search daily on websites or social media groups that supply actors with information on open auditions.

Facebook has a few casting groups that constantly look for actors. Search for castings and auditions in your area on FB and even Instagram or twitter. Always keep your eyes and ears open to those auditioning streets. Know what's going on!

A few Facebook Casting Pages

1. Casting Actors Of Color
2. NYC Casting Calls
3. Lead Casting Call
4. Grant Wilfley Casting
5. Casting Solutions
6. Auditions-Database
7. Atlanta Auditions and Casting Calls
8. Auditions & Casting Calls
9. Casting 360

Subscribe to actorsaccess.com, backstage.com or Mandy.com for more auditions.

    When you get to a certain level as an actor and are now booking roles on network television, premium cable TV shows and premium subscription shows like NETFLIX, you might not want to go to open casting calls or use actors access to find auditions anymore. But networking and forging relationships with industry professionals who are current can help you get into the audition room for even bigger roles and move up the ladder.

How do I network? Where do I go?

    Film festivals, premiers or screenings of films, Sag-AFTRA union meetings, wrap parties of shows or films, casting director meet and greets or classes (always until you're a series regular), agents and manager classes and meet and greets, short or long term acting classes, readings, theater, improv and comedy shows are great ways to network with industry professionals. You must leave your house in order for something to happen and be in the environment of greatness in order for it or an opportunity to rub off on you.

CREATE YOUR OWN WORK

Actors can tend to have a lot of down time depending on their day or night jobs and that down time should be as productive as possible in order to stay in the game and constantly grow. A great way to do that is to create your own work. A lot of actors are constantly waiting for the perfect role to be sent to them by their agents but why not write it yourself? Do you think writing is difficult? It's really not at all. I used to think writing was the world's biggest chore but I figured out this little secret to make it super easy.

I spoke all of the characters lines into my recorder app or pressed the microphone icon in my notes app on my phone. It typed everything I said and in 10 minutes I had 1 page of dialog done. All I did was come up with an idea for a scene, decided on a location, named the 2 characters In that scene, created their objectives so I knew what they were fighting for and what their purpose was and then spoke it all into the recorder. It's easier if you take a scene from your life or something you've experienced in an environment you were in that you think would make an entertaining or compelling story and just re-tell that story buy recording into your notes app on your phone. I've done this for almost all of my sketches, my one-woman show and 1 act plays. I do this walking down the street, on the train and in cafes. It's the easiest way to start writing and from there I usually cut and paste what I created in my notes app and type more where needed and then email it to myself in order to transfer it to final draft or a word doc.

Writing shouldn't be looked at as scary or overwhelming when it comes to creating your own work for 2 reasons. 1) I just gave you a super easy way to write your next work and 2) think of how accomplished you will be once you have created your own work. That should be the drive that pushes you to do this. When nobody is hiring you for a role, create your own. Don't let anybody control your destiny. Once you've written your feature film, sketch, 1 act, play, short film, series, and monologue or web series for yourself, be sure to take it all the way and finish the job. Cast it and produce it with some of your acting tribe and enter it into film festivals like I did with my web series or perform it. Show the world how amazing you are by putting your sketches or series on YouTube or Instagram. What ever you do, don't stop at the writing. Take it all the way. Don't worry about it being perfect just do your best. And don't worry about what people think. Most actors aren't going to do what you do because of laziness and complacency or fear. But you need to set yourself apart by doing everything in your power to make it and become the successful actor of your dreams. And trust me, if you continue to create your own work you will only get better. I've created 3 projects for myself. A short film called "Cool KIdz" about inner city bullying in the Bronx, NY. That film wasn't my best work by any means but I kept going. I then created A one-woman show called, The Closet Bitch where I play 19 characters in 80 minutes and then I turned that play into a 13 episode web series with my talented artist friend and director William Alexander Runnels. We have also entered the series into film festivals; won lots of awards, meetings with big networks and we're getting a lot of attention and growing exponentially because of it! There are so many options for you to create your own work. You just have to make a decision and set a date to do it.

You can also just write an outline of a scene or a sketch and perform it with a friend or fellow actor. An outline is a short summary of what the scene is about. It can be anywhere from a few sentences to a page long. An outline is sometimes enough information and the perfect guide for an actor to be able to improv a scene and even film it with or without other actors. As long as you know the beginning, middle and end of your story you should be able to improvise the scene. Unless you know you're the type of person who needs a clear full out script to follow. If this is the case then I strongly suggest you jump into an improve class and send me a thank you email or DM later. But I've filmed a bazillion sketches that were only outlines and not complete scripts and it usually came out great and I know lots of actors who do the same. The best part is it gave me the freedom to come up with lines I would've never thought of if I had written a script. So much magic happens when you just go with the flow, having a blast, playing at the top of your intelligence and are living and responding in the moment in a scene. That's what improv is all about.

This tool came in handy for my snapchat and instagram videos. I gained more followers and fans from doing improvised character sketches by just deciding what I'm going to talk about or what the scene was. Sometimes I would write it out, and then just pick up my phone and record it with one hand and a clean wall in my background. I'd use IMovie to edit it if I felt it needed editing and in an hour or two later I had content! I created my own work and had a blast while doing it! All you need is some natural light and a good idea!

GET BACK IN CLASS

Weather you jump in a quick 2-4 day intensive for on camera, acting technique, voice, business for actors, improv, commercial or audition technique course or decide to take another acting class or join a theater company for a longer period of time, this will definitely help you to stay in it.

Being around other actors and putting yourself in the environment that forces you to stretch your mind creatively and expand your knowledge on your industry or technique will only help you, refresh your drive and strengthen so many parts of you.

I used to jump in intensives and classes all the time even after I booked co-star and guest starring roles. I'm still in improv class as I write this book and looking to always jump in an amazing acting class with a great teacher. I'm always looking to get better and become stronger and grow my network. The spark that I get from class always reminds me of why I love acting so much. Also to see the drive of my classmates and their desire to become better actors is so inspiring. Always recharge that acting battery if you have to.

BEING AN EXTRA OR STAND-IN

"An Extra" or "Background Actor" is a job in TV or film where actors act in the background of scenes in shoots. It usually doesn't require any speaking unless you get bumped up and usually you aren't seen for more than a few seconds. A lot of the time background actors helps to create the reality of an "exterior" otherwise known as an outside environment shot, or "interior", inside shot, while the camera focuses on the main characters in the scene. Like people walking down the street, sitting on the bus, eating in a restaurant or looking at art in a museum.

There are a lot of opportunities for background actors, like learning about the business side of things and how production works, hearing about upcoming opportunities, getting bumped up to a speaking role, networking and rubbing shoulders with famous actors, directors, writers, show runners, producers and principals while on set.

A stand-in actor is an actor hired to literally stand-in for one of the principal actors in a series or Film. Usually you must be around the same height, weight, complexion and have similar hair texture and color because they usually use stand-in's for setting up shots, lighting, camera angles and this can take quite a long time sometimes and they want the principal actors to spend as much time as they possibly can getting ready and rehearsing for the shot so when the director calls action, everybody's ready to work.

How do I become a Background or Stand-in Actor?

You usually get hired as an extra based off of your look. If it's a mob movie, you most likely wont get cast if you look like a hippie unless they're shooting a hippie scene. But this isn't the case all of the time. Sometime they need massive people for a scene with a large crowd and are casting whoever is available.

In order to become a background actor make sure you have a state ID or drivers license, social security card or passport, be prepared to fill out an I-9 Form (https://www.uscis.gov/i-9) and are allowed to work in the U.S. Have your headshots ready and be prepared to submit more than one headshot because the more looks you provide, the more casting opportunities you will have.

Keep in mind that background actors can work very long hours. I've worked 16 hours as background before. Yes they feed you as well but bring your own snacks just in case. Also be prepared to stand and sit for long hours. You may even be standing or sitting for hours in the rain, snow or heat. But I never complained as an extra about these things because I was so grateful for what I was soaking in and experiencing. I also knew it was a great way to pay my dues as a new actor and a great way to make some extra cash while doing and being surrounded by what I loved.

Actors like Clint Eastwood, Brad Pitt, Matt Damon, Ben Affleck, Renee Zellweger and Meagan Fox were all extras before they were stars.

Sign up here to become a background actor in your area with these sites

*There may be a small registration fee but no one should ever ask you for hundreds of dollars to register in order to become an extra. If they do, it would be wise not to do business with them. I am only giving you information that I have heard good things about or used myself in NYC and LA. Please do your own research on all companies, schools, links and people even if listed in this book to ensure your comfort and peace of mind.

"Remember there are no small parts, only small actors."
– **Constantin Stanislavski**

NEW YORK
http://gwcinyc.com/fancastic.php
https://www.centralcasting.com/register/
https://www.nycastings.com/
http://www.donnagrossmancasting.com/about-us.html
https://www.kipperman.com/
https://www.genuinerealpeople.com/database/

LOS ANGELES
https://www.centralcasting.com/la/talent/
https://www.creativeextrascasting.com/contact
http://www.armstrongcasting.com/about-information
https://www.launcut.com/talent.php

GEORGIA
https://www.centralcasting.com/ga/
https://hyltoncasting.com/submissions/extras/

NEW ORLEANS
https://www.centralcasting.com/nola/
https://couloncasting.com/extras-registration/register/
http://www.bathersoncasting.com/about.htm
https://www.caballerocasting.com/2018/9/10/jm7xvnaby5217lrezxzjxtrqst95pi
https://gloriosocasting.wordpress.com/registration/
https://mycastingfile.com/about/

Also check the trade journals, follow movies on social media that are currently being shot in your area, follow casting agencies on social media and check backstage and actors access.com as well.

You can be a non-union or union background/extra actor. Non-union background actor's get paid less than a union background actor. Union Background gets paid around $170 per day in NY & LA according to the SAG-AFTRA 2018-2019 Handbook. Non-Union pay rates may vary.

What is SAG-AFTRA?

Sag-AFTRA is a Labor union that represents film and television actors, journalists, radio personalities, voice over actors, singers and other media professionals worldwide.

I love being a SAG-AFTRA actor and have been in the union for over 10+ years. I feel protected and covered as an actor knowing my rights are top priority to the Union.

There are 3 ways to become SAG-AFTRA eligible.

1. If you work 3 days as a background actor on a SAG-AFTRA production with a SAG-AFTRA collective bargaining agreement.

2. Work 1 day as a principal or have a speaking role on a SAG-AFTRA production with a SAG-AFTRA collective bargaining agreement.

3. If you are a paid-up member of an affiliated performers' union such as ACTRA, AEA, AGMA or AGVA for a period of one year, and has worked and been paid for at least once as a principal performer in that union's jurisdiction.

HOW I GOT MY SAG-AFTRA CARD!!!!!!!!

I got my SAG-AFTRA card from doing background work on a TV soap opera and few films. I think it was "As The World Turns, "SALT" and "All My Children". I collected working vouchers from each project, took them to the SAG-AFTRA offices, submitted some paperwork and they told me I was sag eligible and all I had to do was pay to join. I think my mother paid around $2,700 at that time for me to join. Bless her soul. We didn't have it like that but she sacrificed and supported my dream and never complained about paying all that money upfront. When I got my SAG-AFTRA card in the mail I celebrated with my mother and felt so accomplished. Getting your SAG-AFTRA card in the mail is a huge step for almost every actor. So stay focused & Hustle to make it happen.

5

Own Your Image

When I say your image, I mean your full package. Your self-representation has to be on point. Clothing, hair, teeth, body odor, the overall first impression a casting director will get before you even open up your mouth is super important.

No matter your size, look, past experiences, or whatever you think might be your flaw can totally be your strength. Remember, you never know what casting directors, directors, producers and agents are looking for. But whatever you do, be YOU. Your authentic self needs to shine so do what makes you comfortable and happy as long as you're not disrespecting anyone. Rock your natural hair, rock your died hair, rock those extensions, own your body type and style and be proud of it!

Walk in every room being totally comfortable and confident with who you are because that is what will ultimately get you cast.

You are the prize, you are the business.

You must remember that you are the prize here. Producers, directors, writers, casting directors and agents need YOU to tell their stories and make their jobs and lives easier and most of all..

Make them MONEY! There are many different types of roles and characters to play. You will have many opportunities to play the role that fits your "product" or "brand" and that's where you will shine and hopefully book lots of work because of how well you "own it".

Confidence is KEY. Owning the skin you're in can help everyone see what your brand is and it allows you to fully concentrate on your craft and the business when your auditioning, meeting with industry professionals or networking.

Do not over think this or try to be someone that you're not. Never loose yourself to the hustle. Stay true to YOU. Too many people in this industry hurt themselves in the process of trying to be better looking, slimmer, thicker, taller, clearer skin, more muscular, straighter teeth, longer or shorter hair, and all those things are fine as long as that's what YOU want and not what you think will get you hired. The most important thing is to go about it in healthy way with a positive attitude.

Right now, right where you are, I want you to love and embrace who you are and own it by looking in the mirror and saying these words..

> *"I am enough, I am uniquely me, I forgive myself for not realizing how amazing I am and not giving myself enough credit. I love who I am and I am grateful and happy to be me. Thank you for this moment and thank you for all that I am."*

My girlfriend calls this "Mirror Work". Whenever I feel down or less than (which happens to the best of us) I do my mirror work and sometimes it works right away and sometimes it doesn't. But when

I continue to do it, it eventually works! I start to see how blessed and amazing I am. My back gets straighter and my confidence skyrockets!! If you stick with your mirror work it will only bring you to a better place with self. Come up with your own mantra of what you want to say in the mirror and give yourself the gift of constantly reprogramming your mind to own the skin you're in and if you must change anything about yourself for the better, do it while loving and appreciating who you are every step of the way as you accomplish your goals.

I remember trying to loose weight and constantly picking at my belly fat and body shaming myself in the mirror and literally hating what I saw. My father always told me how chunky I was and made it very clear regardless of who was around just how much weight I gained and would crack a few jokes. So appreciating my body was one of the hardest things for me to learn how to do. I still struggle with it sometimes. But I started to reprogram my mind and say how beautiful my body was and although I'd like to loose 20 pounds for comfort and health I am grateful for what I have, who I am and I love every inch of ME. It would put me in a happier more positive mental state, which made it easier for me to turn down certain foods and only eat what made me feel good and what was good for me in addition to actually wanting to exercise.

> *"If there's any message to my work, it is ultimately that it's OK to be different, that we should question ourselves before we pass judgment on someone who looks different, behaves different, is a different color."* – **Johnny Depp**

> *"Respect has always been top priority for me. Respect of myself and respect of others. Respect mixed with discipline and goals makes you rare and powerful."* **-Shana Solomon**

"Overcome the notion that you must be regular. It robs you of the chance to be extraordinary." – **Uta Hagen**

Learn how to become a SAG-AFTRA "Union" Actor by visiting this link.

https://www.sagaftra.org/membership-benefits/steps-join

6

Your Mental Health

"The actor has to develop his body. The actor has to work on his voice. But the most important thing an actor has to work on is his mind." – **Stella Adler**

I cannot stress enough how super important it is for an actor to have a healthy positive mindset. With the amount of effort, work, discipline, energy, willpower, time, drive and supreme self-confidence it takes to "make it" in this business, the one thing that will and must remain strong and healthy is your MIND.

Of course you will and are allowed to have bad and sucky moments and days, this is life. Shit happens. We can't control everything nor can we control what other people do that may affect our world but we do have complete control over our mental state by controlling what we choose to think about, what we say, listen to and what we focus on.

I had a day where I was not only late to an audition but did terrible on an audition that I worked so hard for and then to top it all off, got my brand new IPhone stolen right out of my hand on the metro-north, which is supposed to be the "nice train" in NYC. Spent most of my evening in a police station and then came home hoping I'd catch up on my "Game of Thrones" and realized my cable was cut off and I didn't have the money to pay for it. So yeah, I've had a crazy and emotionally draining day before and have also had way worse. Like when I didn't get an audition after that for a few months and had all kinds of other bad things happen to me during that time. So imagine what was going on in my mind about acting, about my life, my goals and how I could've felt that my career was slipping through my fingers by the day. Imagine not booking a single role and never getting a callback in an entire year after going on almost 50+ auditions. What do you think that could do to your mind? How do you think you would feel? I've been there. But as I said before, these are the beautiful times. These moments and feelings are very possible but they can and will make you super strong, if you turn every adversity and painful moment into a lesson and counter it with positive thoughts and actions and be patient for the storm to clear because it will.

When you experience something that doesn't feel good, generally people might then follow that feeling with a thought and then negative self-talk. For example, say you did horrible at your audition. As soon as you leave the casting directors office you might think to yourself how bad it went and how "off" you were and start to question yourself and your acting ability. You will start to replay the entire audition in your mind moment after terrible moment over and over again until you start to say out loud or to yourself "I'm a terrible actor! I suck at auditioning! Why do I even do this to myself? I should've done this; I should've done that! I rushed; I didn't even listen, what happened in there? That's not how I rehearsed it! I don't think this acting this is for me anymore." So now you are reinforcing the pain and adding more negativity to the situation and most of all to your mind. Believe it or not this is an affirmation as well. It's just a negative one. Weather you feed your mind positive or negative thoughts, whichever one you spend your time thinking and speaking and focusing on will become your reality. As a man thinketh, so shall he become.

Eventually your negative self talk about how terrible you are at auditioning could possibly lead you to taking negative action or sending out negative vibrations and cause you to begin to live the life of an actor who is actually terrible at auditioning. You might eventually just quit acting all together, which is the ultimate worst thing you could ever do! If acting is your passion and it's one of the main things that makes you happy and brings you joy and fulfills you and gives you purpose, sets your soul free and on fire at the same time, then why would you allow a bad audition or not getting an audition for a year cause you to give up on YOU and what YOU LOVE TO DO and what brings YOU JOY? A great actor by the name of John Barrymore said, "A man is not old until regrets take the place of dreams." Do you see how far this negative and unhealthy mindset can spiral all the way down into quitting or doubting yourself, which can lead to depression? So don't ever let a bad moment or day or week or the inaction of others, or what others think of you cause you to think badly about yourself or less than and give up on yourself or your dreams and goals. You are enough. Your time will come. Stay focused. Persist until you succeed. But take the time you need to heal.

One of my great girlfriend's, who's name I'd like to keep private so I'll call her Sylvia. Sylvia was having one of those years. Sylvia hadn't booked anything in over a year and was feeling depressed. Sylvia, like me, was working a job that she hated because it took up a lot of her time and would make it very difficult for her to audition or even prepare for an audition. It was one of those soul-sucking jobs that can rob you of every ounce of happiness if you allow it to. Many actors who work a 9-5 or like I did, have a night job Bartending or serving can tend to "over work" and not set boundaries with their work schedules or didn't choose a job that allows them the freedom and money needed to put the necessary time and finances into their acting careers in order to grow. Sylvia's job was literally weighing her down, effecting everything around her including her relationships and she felt super stuck and stagnant in her acting career.

I personally have experienced being at work behind an extremely busy bar one night and received an audition from my agent on my phone around 6pm. Now 6pm is prime time for bars because everyone's just getting off work and ready for that cocktail. Mind you, this audition was for the next day at 3pm for an amazing role but I wasn't going to get off until 3am, get home at 4am and study as much as possible which was probably till like 5 am, to wake up at 10am study some more, get ready at 12pm, leave my house between 1 and 1:30pm to take the bus and the train and travel an hour and half to get to my audition at 3pm. Was I well rested and ready to conquer my audition? No. Did I feel prepared, memorized, and make some awesome character choices for my audition? Nah. Did I bomb at my audition? You know it!! And on top of all that, having an insane amount of anxiety because I knew I had to call and ask my manager if I can come in late because the audition cut into my travel time to get to work and of course this manager didn't give a shit about my acting career. All he cared about was up-selling high end liquor to customers and bottle sales.

So back to Sylvia, she ended up booking a TV role, not the role she wanted but booked something. And she became extremely happy for a few days. But when filming was over and she had to go back to work Sylvia's depression started to creep back in. Sylvia realized she was allowing the fact that she hadn't booked an acting job due to her soul sucking job, to control her happiness which ultimately made her feel insecure and she didn't book anything after that for a while. She realized that she didn't like how much control the outcome of an audition had over her self worth. She also realized she wasn't auditioning much and barely booking because of her job and mental state. Sylvia was doing herself a huge disservice by not working the type of job that would support her acting career. She was also constantly telling herself that she hated her job, which only made things worse. But Sylvia was too scared of change, she feared not finding another job that would afford her current lifestyle and honestly, she just didn't think there was a job out there that would support her acting career. So Sylvia continued focusing on negative thoughts that didn't serve her which brought her further down into depression.

But things changed. Sylvia revamped her resume and when she got an interview for a job she let them know right off the back that she's an actor who might have to suddenly go to an audition or may be late from time to time or switch shifts and would always give them notice and insured them that she would handle all of her responsibilities as long as she is able to take the time she needs for her acting career. Sylvia finally found the perfect job! Well not perfect but they were really understanding about her needs as an actor and understood that her acting career came first. She had to cut back on a few things and make some lifestyle changes like, no cable TV, not eat out as much or hang out the way she used to but it was all worth it. Sylvia's vibe got lighter and more positive. She started writing in what she calls her "gratitude journal" everyday. She would write everything she was grateful for as soon as she woke up and it started to change her outlook on life. At first, she didn't book any roles although she went on tons of auditions. But after every audition, no matter if she bombed or did amazing, she would leave it in the room. Meaning she would let it go! Sylvia decided to say, "Whatever is meant to be, will be and what is for me is for me. I will book the role of my dreams very soon." Sylvia also started to say daily affirmations like, "I'm booking a recurring role on.....(very specific TV series) and winning awards". She put her ego aside and hung out with her acting friends who were booked and busy, she would ask them questions and learn from their experiences. She started to read positive, motivating stories about famous actors and their struggles, started a blog and began speaking up on issues that affected her community. This helped her grow her instagram page to super high numbers and become an ambassador for products for girls just like her. Sylvia started having fun with her life, tapping into other interests and hobbies and doing what made her happy and in return it gave her more purpose. But ultimately she did all these things to stay in it and keep a positive mind frame to attract and be prepared for that perfect role of her dreams. She wasn't going to quit acting just because things weren't going "her way" or the way she envisioned it. I bullshit you not, Sylvia ended up booking that recurring role on that (very specific TV series) She worked on the show for years and attended the 23rd annual Screen Actors Guild (SAG) awards because the show was nominated and won! This role has opened many doors for Sylvia. Sylvia has never been so calm and at peace with her position as a working actor as she is now. But let's not forget that her journey was a bit rough. And she still has a ways to go. But also keep in mind that I didn't tell you all that she went through to get here, only a small piece of the story was given.

Sometimes we think the journey will be super straight and smooth, but what fun would that be? How will we truly learn and grow from the easy road in? Embrace the rough and windy road. It will make you not only the ultimate hustler like Sylvia but it will make you a better version of yourself.

Here is what you can do to keep your mind healthy & positive

1) Do a self-check in

When you start to think negative thoughts about your current situation, it's really good to be aware of your own bullshit. I say bullshit because you are slowly talking yourself out of believing that you can achieve your goals and dreams and that you aren't worthy of them. This will become true if you don't stop it and start to flip it.

Once you say to yourself "okay, I'm currently feeding myself more negative talk which will only bring me down," make a choice no matter how difficult or phony it may seem at the time, to tell yourself something positive and think positive thoughts. For example, instead of harping on an audition that didn't go so well for days and weeks, Sylvia started to leave auditions saying, "whatever happens happens! I'm a star either way and the perfect role for me is coming very soon." And then she would treat herself to a cappuccino and sit in a cool café and let it all go. If Sylvia continued to have auditions that didn't go so well, she would jump in an audition technique class or an on camera class like a good 'ol amazing Bob Krakower class, and brush up on her skills. So both affirming positive thoughts and taking positive actions transformed Sylvia's mindset from thinking negative thoughts that will only lead to a negative downward spiral, into personal growth and better energy to not only be around but she will most likely naturally attract another audition or an opportunity to do something awesome. I truly believe the thoughts we have in our minds, send out energy waves into the universe and we will naturally attract things that are in alignment with those thoughts. So, why not have a more positive outlook on life? I totally get being chipper and skipping down the street with the world's widest smile isn't always the mood we're in but we don't have to think like a Debbie downer either and honestly that's the quickest way to live a miserable life and have a very unsuccessful acting career. So be aware of your own negative thoughts as soon as you think them and be aware of your negative self talk and make a decision to flip it with positive thoughts and affirmations. Tell yourself "it's okay, everything is a learning lesson and obviously I had to learn something from this experience. I am an amazing actor and most of all an amazing human being who continues to grow and learn about life. I will also continue to grow and learn about my craft to become an even more amazing actor and I am reaching all of my goals. I am booking the perfect role for me. I am grateful for even knowing what my calling is and grateful to be able to do it. Thank you." And go treat yourself to a walk in the park, a phone call to someone you miss, a movie or whatever makes you genuinely feel pure joy. Go be good to YOU.

2) Meditate & Visualize

Meditation is a practice where an individual uses a technique such as focusing their mind on a particular object, thought or activity to train attention and awareness, and achieve a mentally clear and emotionally calm and stable state.

What a lot of my friends and I do when we mediate is we wait until we are alone and in a completely quiet and calm environment like our homes, sit in a chair or floor, lay on the floor or anywhere you feel you can sit or lay for a long period of time. I usually sit in the chair in my living room and face the window and allow the sun to shine on my face and body. We decide what we will meditate on. We might need clarity on a situation or want to start our day off energized and motivated by visualizing ourselves living our best lives after reaching our biggest goals. Or we might just want to bring our anxiety levels down and calm our energy so we may decide to visualize ourselves sitting on a quiet beach in a hammock while the ocean breeze blows across our skin as we listen to the waves brush the sand. The goal is to feel good, better, clearer, more energized, focused or peaceful. So setting an intention before you meditate is super important. Once we've decided what we want to focus on when we mediate, we set our timers anywhere from 10-30 minutes. You can set it for as long as you like but I suggest starting out with at least 10 minutes. It might be weird at first to just sit in silence and you will probably start itching and fidgeting and you may feel your eyes jumping and you might even see or have bad thoughts and visions pop up in your mind at first but this is all apart of your body and mind resisting and fighting change. Meditation helps you grow by learning about what's going on inside of you and teaches you how to quiet the noise in your mind that you pick up every second from your daily environment. So now we are ready to press start on the timer and close our eyes. It's really good to hone in your focus and energy by taking deep breaths by breathing in deeply with your nose, holding it for 2-3 seconds and slowly breathing out through your mouth. Don't be afraid to let a little noise out when you exhale. Do this 5-8 times and then begin to breathe effortlessly. This helps to release tension. Once you feel the tension, anxiety or fear has decreased even if just a little, start to visualize by focusing on what you want by seeing, feeling, being, smelling, tasting the experiences. See yourself looking and feeling amazing as you go to your audition, feel prepared that you know your lines and what choices your going to make in the room, see yourself doing amazing and the casting director is shaking their head in amazement and tells you how fantastic of a job you did. Hear your agent telling you with excitement in his or her voice that you booked the role! And to look out for an email for your offer. See yourself on set sitting in your cast chair with your name on it. Feel the heat from the bright studio lights hitting your skin as your acting in a film. Fell the joy of watching production set up the shot for the next scene while your speaking with other cast members about life or what's going on in the scene. Feel hair and make up prepare you for your series regular role. Smell your food from crafty (food service for film & TV productions) on set while eating it inside your personal trailer that comes with a couch, a microwave, it's own bathroom and closet. Hear the door knock and the PA (production assistant) call your name to set. Feel you living in the moment under imaginary circumstances while acting on set and then hear everyone say what a great job you did. This is how I as well some of my acting tribe get what we want. We visualize what we want, weather we feel great or bad but especially when we feel bad. We reset our minds to feeling, smelling, touching and seeing what we want by closing our eyes and putting ourselves there. By the time we open our eyes we are untouchable and unstoppable. Because we actually experienced it in our minds. We are ready to seize the day and have a better outlook on things because we are now in a high vibrational positive state. It's also amazing how many ideas come from mediating and visualizing. Allow your mind to travel to other positive places and be open to what you discover. We have written books, blogs, made movies, web series, came up with amazing characters all from this exercise. The example I gave you is just one of the ways we strengthen our positive thoughts and energy and turn our bad moments or days around. You can visualize whatever you want as long as it's positive and healthy for you.

Hopefully you have done your vision board or have plans to do one ASAP so you can have a clear visual as to what your life looks like when you achieve your goals. This will definitely help you with your meditation.

3) Follow Inspirational pages and profiles on Social media

Sometimes reading a few simple quotes on instagram or watching a quick motivational video on YouTube can put me right back on track to positive healthy thinking. Use hashtags like #positiveaffirmations, #Motivation, #Inspiration, #Positiveenergy, #Inspirationalquotes, #Quotes, #hustle #goals #lovewhatyoudo or #passion on Instagram or Facebook. Search "Motivational videos", "Best inspirational videos" on YouTube or Facebook. Type in inspirational speakers names in the YouTube search bar like, Jim Rohn, Lisa Nichols, Wayne Dyer, Les Brown, Gary Vaynerchuck, who happen to be some of my faves and helped me during dark and depressing times. Follow, like and subscribe to those inspirational pages and profiles so you can get alerts whenever a new post video is released. You never know, you might get that alert for the perfect video when you need it most. Happens to me allll the time. This can be a little perfect dose of daily inspiration for you weather you're on the go or are swamped with studying and other work. These quotes and vids can quickly reset your mind and flip bad thoughts and self talk into positive ones.

4) Connect with your Positive supporters

Who ever supports you and your dreams without judgment are the people or person you should call when times get rough and you need a little pick me up. Weather it's family, friends, a therapist, a classmate or a co-worker, if this person has great positive energy and you have seen them flip a negative situation into a positive one and you trust this person to give you great advice and because they genuinely love or support and respect you and they are honest, feel free to open up to this person about what you are going through and allow them to help you.

Reaching out and seeking guidance and help from those you trust can be a healthy thing for the simple fact that it's good to just vent and get those confusing, troubling or negative thoughts that have been boggled up in your mind out. Venting and talking to those you trust can release worry, fear and anxiety and help you see things more clear. Don't you usually feel better after you speak to a friend or family member when something's bothering you? I do, when it's someone I trust of course. So ask the person you trust if it's okay if you call them every now and then when your going through something and need someone to just listen and talk to, if they say yes then please take action and actually reach out to them when you do go through something that's upsetting you or negatively affecting you. I'm sure this person will welcome you with open arms if you make it clear that you need them. I used to do this a lot but I have gotten to the point where I now dig deep within self and flip it on my own unless something earth shattering happens like when I lost my mom. But when I'm just having a bad moment and feeling down and overwhelmed, I turn to me, a quote, a book, video or song and I flip it on my own. I pick and choose my venting sessions because you never know when the person you normally turn to for advice needs advice themselves or needs some space. So yes, it's great to reach out to those who love and support you but the goal is to get stronger and better at flipping negative situations and thoughts into positive ones so you can be your own strength and also become that helping hand and beacon of light for someone else who really needs it. That is the ultimate position to be in, a position where you are actually able to help someone get to a better place in life because you have done it for yourself.

5) Listen to Music

Listening to music can change almost anyone's mood instantaneously. There's something magical that happens inside of us when we hear an amazing melody combined with the perfect words we needed to hear to uplift our spirits that our hearts and minds connect to like magnets. My song used to be "I just wanna be Successful" by Drake and Eminem's, "Loose yourself". I would play these songs repeatedly until they seeped into my subconscious and became affirmations. There are so many songs that can uplift you when you feel down or need a little inspiration. Search "best inspirational songs" or "motivational music" in Google or YouTube and see what you find. You might find a song you know and when you listen to it again, when you need it most, you will realize it hits your soul differently. It will be even more powerful.

Create a playlist with at least 20 songs that gets you pumped up before or after auditions and positive life changing moments in your life. Create a playlist that will uplift your spirits and inspire you to keep pushing. Create any playlist you want and need to help you flip negative thoughts into positive ones. Music seeps into our subconscious and can turn our entire mood around in under 5 minutes. This almost always works for me as well as so many successful actors. Be sure to title your playlists with something that will inspire you and remind you that this is the playlist that you NEED to listen to right now. Make sure these playlists are on your phone or a device that you can carry with you so you can listen to them on the spot whenever you need them.

6) Cry It Out

I'm not big on harping on what I can't control. A lot of what we do as actors depends on other people's decisions. All we can do is be the best version of ourselves and continue to work on that, kill every role we get no matter what obstacles were faced with, have goals and dreams, have a plan in place to accomplish those goals and dreams and take action the smartest way by hustling our asses off until we reach those goals and obtain those dreams. However, the plan doesn't always go the way we visualize it. So when life throws rocks and boulders on your smooth path to your dreams, you have to lean how to step over or move around them instead of jackhammering them like a mad man until they dissolve.

The goal is to learn to let go of what you can't control and hustle and focus on what you can from a mentally positive place. So if I feel super emotional or upset about something that I can't control and it's hard to let it go or walk away from, It's usually because I'm emotionally attached to someone, something or some idea and once I realize I'm emotionally attached and I'm hurt because I did all I could do and it's still not going "my way" or how I expected it to, I usually feel like I want to cry. So I do. And when I do, I ball like the most dramatic character on a novella I've rolled allover my floor, went to go look at myself in the mirror just to cry and do the ugly face in the mirror and be even more dramatic, stomp and scream all over the house and punch pillows. This is all done when I'm alone of course. But I feel sooo much better and lighter and clearer when I'm done releasing. Sometimes we just have to scream and cry and let out that stuffy overwhelming emotional energy in order to let things go. When was the last time you cried? Check in with self right now about anything that may be bothering you or giving you anxiety. Does the thought of that thing fill you up with overwhelming emotion? If it does, go to a bathroom or wait until you get home or in an environment where you feel comfortable letting it out and just cry and scream about it for as long as you have to. Girls let the eyeliner and mascara run until you turn into a raccoon and guys be free, it's okay. We're all human and need to cry every now and then so just remind yourself that you are allowed to cry and that it's okay to be HUMAN. This will help you with the start of flipping the negative thoughts you had about a situation into positive ones.

7) Read Self-Help Books Or Listen To the Audio

As I mentioned in chapter 4, books have the necessary information to teach us how to learn what we need in order to raise our value and knowledge on a specific topic. Why not learn to become a better version of yourself by learning how to become a stronger more mentally healthy and positive human being? I'm telling you, great energy goes a looong way in this business so get your energy right by working from within and a great way to start to do that is by picking up a book.

Here's a list of 24 of the best self help and mind strengthening books that have helped me and many other people flip their negative thoughts and situations into positive ones.

1. The Greatest Salesman in The World By, Og Mandino
2. The 4 Agreements By, Don Miguel Ruiz
3. The Mastery Of Self By, Don Miguel Ruiz
4. Think and Grow Rich By, Napoleon Hill
5. How To Win Friends & Influence people By, Dale Carnegie
6. The Art of Happiness By, HH The Dalai Lama

7. As A Man Thinketh By, James Allen
8. A Year of Positive Thinking By, Cyndie Spiegel
9. Year of Yes By, Shonda Rhimes
10. Girl, wash Your Face By, Rachel Hollis
11. The Art of Asking: How I learned to stop worrying and let people help By, Amanda Palmer
12. The Universe Has Your Back: Transform Fear to Faith By, Gabrielle Bernstein
13. The 7 Habits Of Highly Effective People BY, Stephen R. Covey
14. The 4-Hour Work Week By, Timothy Ferris
15. Getting Things Done: The Art of Stress-Free Productivity By, David Allen
16. The Road Less Traveled By, M. Scott Peck
17. Man's Search For Meaning By, Viktor E. Frankl
18. The Power of Now By, Eckhart Tolle
19. The life-Changing Magic of Tidying Up: The Japanese Art of De-cluttering and Organizing By, Marie Kondo
20. The Subtle Art of Not Giving A F*ck By, Mark Manson
21. The Happiness Project By, Gretchen Rubin
22. You Are A Badass: How to Stop Doubting Your Greatness And Start Living An Awesome Life By, Jen Sincero
23. The 10X Rule By, Grant Cardone
24. The Alchemist By, Paulo Coelho

8) Positive Affirmations

Please review Chapter 4 but these bad boys saved my life. I noticed it saved some of my friends' lives as well and helped them turn negative thinking into positive living. My girlfriend used to always say "I'm so broke, I have no money, I can't do anything unless it's free so don't call me if it costs." She now says "I'm working on my finances right now and in one year I will have reached my goal of being financially independent and can go anywhere I damn well please." She has a new job and makes almost 20 thousand dollars more than she did 6 months ago! What a great start to her goal! We both believe she is attracting more money due to the affirmations she says which flipped her negative thoughts about her financial situation into positive ones.

Here's a list of motivational affirmations & quotes to live by

1. I take action everyday to become a better actor.
2. Everyday I hustle toward my goals.
3. I believe in my greatness and myself.
4. I'm motivated by my goals and aware of my fears but my goals always outweigh my fears because I know they are not my reality.
5. I deserve everything I want and dream about.
6. I'm making it happen no matter what!
7. I'm an amazing actor.
8. I'm a successful actor.
9. I will Persist until I succeed.
10. My Passion Is Acting.

11. I pay all of my bills from acting and live the life I want to live from my amazing acting jobs.

12. I attract the best most powerful roles that make me a better actor and allow me to continue to get great work and forge amazing relationships

13. I get everything I desire.

9) EXERCISE

Every single time I feel down or depressed or any type of doubt or fear, getting off of my ass and going for a simple walk usually helps me feel better. There's something about fresh air and moving the body that relieves stress and helps clear the mind. I know that actually getting out of the bed can be and feel like one of the hardest things to do when we feel down or if you live in New York and it's 25 degrees outside. But you must remember your goals don't care one bit about your feelings. The day is still moving and opportunities are out there and available to you and there are always going to be people who will try to outwork you who want it just as bad as you do and will push past their feelings and go get it. However I do believe we always need to take time for ourselves, listen to our bodies and do exactly what we need for our mental health as long as we're not hurting ourselves or anyone else so take the time you need to relax but understand there is a fine line between taking your time and taking too much time.

When I broke up with my boyfriend of 10 years I remember being on my living room couch for 30 days straight, barely eating, crying constantly, writing emo poetry, watching every rom-com on NETFLIX and avoiding fun with my friends like they were infected with Ebola. But I started to get sick of myself. I couldn't take how pitiful and frail I felt. So I got up one day and hopped on my treadmill and jogged a mile. This was the beginning of me getting back to ME and getting out of that "feeling sorry for myself, break up fog". The act of jogging and vigorously moving every muscle in my body at an intense rate made me feel alive again! It helped me clear my head and that's when I started to set new goals for myself and I began to focus on my passion again rather than the loss of love that wasn't healthy for me to begin with. Ever heard of "runners high"? It's a state of euphoria and reduced anxiety and it lessens the ability to feel pain that you can tend to feel after exercising for long periods of time. This "high" is actually your brain releasing endorphins. Endorphins are chemicals that make you feel good and happy. I'm telling you, exercise can really help you feel amazing and happy, put your life into perspective and become more driven to take positive action. So the next time you find yourself curling up on the couch or in bed because you feel depressed or down, remember that taking a walk, going to the gym, jogging, or even doing jumping jacks in the house will help you feel a lot better and just might be the start you need to getting you right back on track.

10) Eat Healthy

Ever eat some greasy fast food meal that you were craving like a mad man but as soon as that last bite really settles you realize that was the biggest mistake of the day? I've done it a bazillion times and have decided I rather feel good after I eat. I also have a goal of playing a superhero in a franchise film or TV series and superhero's usually tend to be fit and healthy. Also, processed and unhealthy foods make you sluggish due to the amount of grease, fat, sugar and lack of nutrients, vitamins and minerals your body needs for fuel and energy. So if you want to be fit and toned it all starts with eating healthy. I think a huge part of mental health is how we feel about ourselves. Depending on what your personal body and health goals are your eating should support them. I know it can be difficult to cut out all "bad" foods, I surely don't but I do eat them in moderation. So, treat yourself to that pint of ice cream one night but then give it a break for a few weeks and make sure you work out. Try your best to do 30 minutes of cardio or exercise 3-5 times per week depending on your body. You should speak to your doctor about what's best for you before making any adjustments.

11) Rest

Some people think that sleep is the cousin of death. I actually think insomnia and sleep deprivation is. We all need down time, relaxation and days where we do absolutely nothing where we kick back and binge watch shows and movies and spend time with the ones we love. Down time and rest is what makes us hustle even harder. When we reward ourselves with a break it recharges our brains and bodies which gives us more energy to push ourselves when it's go time during those times we have to hustle like beasts.

Like for example, it's pilot season and you have 4 auditions in one week or when you're on set for 12+ hours, taking an intensive acting class or studying your lines and rehearsing for opening night. Rest should be the cousin of life. It is a healthy, much needed recharge we need in order to stay alert and productive. If you over work the mind and body, they will eventually shut down and then how will you be able to work those awesome acting jobs? So again, balance and moderation is important here because oversleeping and not doing anything for long periods of time will create the habit of laziness and complacency. Maybe scheduling downtime with your friends, your significant other or family on the weekends or a few times per month might help you create that balance. Another way to rest and relax is to find a series or a film to watch at least once a month and kick back and enjoy some YOU time while you stay current on what's happening in your industry. Or actually take a vacation. But please make sure you get at least 7 hours of sleep every night. That way, you can wake up early to seize the day!

12) Clear Your Mind of Worry & Doubt

In addition to the unexpected, wild and crazy things that can happen in our lives which cause us to worry, the business of entertainment can not only add to it if you allow it to but it can make you doubt yourself. When you worry and feel doubtful about anything in life you should always ask yourself, "Can I do anything about it? Can I control the outcome?" If you can't, you should let it go and allow God or the universe or whatever source you believe in, to handle it and trust that everything will be just fine because this is something you needed to experience and it will help you grow and eventually pass. If you can do something about your current situation and control it, then figure out the best way how by talking to someone you trust or connecting with your source (self or higher power) and decide how you are going to fix it. But there's absolutely no use or help in spending time to worry about anything to the point where you will end up on your couch in the fetus position for 30 days like I was, wasting time and missing out on life's opportunities. So if there's anything currently weighing on you and giving you anxiety because you want the situation to be different then figure out right now if you can actually do anything to make the situation better, if you can, you know what to do. If you can't please give yourself the permission to let it go and cry it out or talk it out if you have to and release it. I read somewhere that worrying is just reliving the moment over and over. Why would you want to relive a moment that didn't feel good over and over? It sounds like something that can make you sick eventually.

And when it comes to self-doubt, revisit those affirmations and self-help books I recommended. It might take some time to build your confidence but please know that you are so amazing and have been blessed with a passion and a dream by a force that would have never given you this blessing unless you were able to obtain it. If you persist, you will succeed. Everything takes it's own special time and sometimes it's not up to us as to how long it takes or how we will get there. But if you stay consistent, you will get there. Also, the mirror work helps wonders with doubt and spending time with people who praise and support you.

13) Self love & Care

This is my favorite thing to do. Self love and care is literally doing positive things that makes you happy and brings you joy. Like going dancing, going to a comedy club, taking cool risks, go kart racing, going to the spa, getting a massage, going to a fancy restaurant, buying yourself something nice, going to the museum, taking a trip, hanging with friends. This helps us feel better and usually brightens up our day. Why not do what you need to do to put a smile on your face? Treat yourself with the same respect and care and thoughtfulness as you do for others. You are the most important person in your life. You deserve it.

14) Hobbies and anything else other than Acting.

I know this book is all about how to hustle as an actor and get your foot in the door in TV and film so you can start making money but a little piece of important advice a very smart woman told me years ago was, "You have to have a life outside of acting or else it will control you." She was so right! My entire world was acting for years but I realized I was kind of becoming a robot when I would go on auditions. I also realized how difficult it was to relate to characters because my life was so cut off from the real world. I judged my characters instead of understanding them and my cool ass, down to earth personality was fading. I didn't have much to talk about and definitely wasn't relatable. I wasn't enjoying life with the people I loved, barely saw my friends and family and I was afraid to go on vacations and experience the world because I thought I might miss an opportunity to audition and book the biggest role of my life. I didn't realize I was currently missing out on the most important role in my life, which was living life itself. Living in the moment is a very important thing an actor must learn to do while acting. If you are premeditating what will happen in a scene then that means it makes no sense for any other actors to be there because you have already decided what's going to happen. You aren't listening or breathing or living in the moment. You're absent of the now and in your own world of what you believe is happening, which the audience calls "BAD ACTING". That is what happens when you do the same thing in real life, you are "BAD LIVING" when you forget or choose not to be in the present moment. You aren't truly listening to people and taking them in and appreciating life in front of you. Do you realize how much we miss when we don't live in the present moment? It is okay if you take time out of your day to focus on something or someone else other than acting. Honestly you should absolutely take time out of your day and focus on something or someone else other than acting. What do you like to do? Or what did you like to do before you became obsessed with acting? Read? Listen to podcasts? Shop? Do makeup? Scroll on the Internet for cars? Fix things? Shoot Pool? Do hair? Tell jokes? Write? I want you to come up with 2 things that you like or liked to do before acting took a hold of your world and make plans to do at least one of them within the next 30 days and commit to it. We all need experiences in life doing different things.

Open up your world to the possibilities. Trust me, even though this is all about not focusing on acting, it will only help you become a better actor and probably attract more auditions, roles and opportunities because you will be doing something that makes you happy and happiness attracts more happiness.

*"Life beats us down and crushes the soul and art reminds you that you have one." – **Stella Adler***

7

You Did That!!!!!!

Congratulations! You are a freaking winner! Pat yourself on the back and tell yourself how amazing you are for coming this far, learning the hustle that it takes to make it in the acting business and finishing this book!

Not many people can finish what they start but you did! So for that I just want to say thank you.

My last piece of advice to you is please don't hustle for greed, hustle for need. When you hustle for greed, you will never be satisfied because greed grows and festers like an infected wound and takes over your mind and you will never be grateful for what you have. When you have a positive need to be great at something, that keeps you alive and growing and without growth our spirits begin to die.

Ever see people walking around in the street looking half dead? It's because they have decided to stop growing, learning from life's lessons and setting goals and have very little to look forward to.

They rather except their current state as the finish line and have decided to give up.

Please, never become a part of the give up crew. If you keep pushing and focus on the NEED to grow and become better and better constantly, there is a finish line filled with so many moments of happiness and gratitude so keep setting new goals and make sure you stop and appreciate your achievements and throw a damn party every time you accomplish a new goal.

As a bonus, I have included a QnA to help you discover and reach your goals, learn and decide how to set action steps on a daily, weekly or monthly basis to achieve those goals in order to get your foot in the door and become a working actor. I'm helping you to start right from where you are and begin to hustle these acting goals. We as actors can have many days of not knowing what to do and can end up feeling stuck and helpless and spending most of our time working, not knowing where to start, hoping an audition or an opportunity lands on our laps or wishing we could do something to move forward. Well, I want you to take each action that you come up with and put it into your calendar weather it's hanging on your wall or on your phone. This will put you in the position to go find the opportunity and grab it by the horns and make things happen for yourself much faster.

The awesome thing about my Actors Hustle QnA is that no matter where you are in your acting career, even if you haven't even started yet, or if you're finished with school, ready to get new representation, looking for auditions and are ready to take your career to the next level, it will allow you to jump in right where you are and be super clear on what your most important goal(s) is and what needs to be done in order to reach that goal(s). But don't procrastinate. As soon as you finish with this final chapter jump right into filling out your QnA Goal setting sheet and put a date to those goals in your Calendar so you can know where your going and when to take action. It's best to take action while you're inspired so be sure to stay consistent with it until you form the new habit of hustling till you reach your goals!

So again, once you know where you are in your career and have decided on what your goal(s) is and what steps need to be taken in order to reach it and fill out your calendar with your daily, weekly, monthly actions, do your absolute best to take that action and accomplish as many steps as you possibly can. And remember, It's okay if you can't afford every class, book, subscription, seminar or meet & greet I list, but it's important to do as much as you can so you can set yourself apart from those who do the bare minimum so you will be noticed, respected grow and win!

Now it's time to say goodbye but hello to a new way of looking at life and your career!

I also must say thank you from the bottom of my heart for reading my book and I hope this information is as useful to you as it was and still is to so many others and me. Use it wisely with full positive intention, I appreciate you.

Now go be great!

P.S. Hustle your ass off and I'll see you at the top.

The Actors Hustle QnA Workbook.

These next few questions will help guide you to knowing exactly what you want, getting super clear with your goals and the steps you need to take in order to achieve them.

Writing "I am" instead of I can or I want to or I need to, is more powerful because it confirms to self that "you will" do exactly what you say you will do and achieve it. "I am" sends a powerful message to the conscious and subconscious mind. It leaves no room for confusion or excuses. It helps you make it happen and get things done.

1) Based on the information you've been reading, I want you to ask yourself, what action will I take after reading this book?????

For example: After reading The Actor's hustle, "I am" going to research and find the best acting school for me.

Write all the things you are going to do and inspired to do here:

I am

_____
_____
_____
_____
_____
_____
_____
_____
_____
_____
_____
_____
_____
_____
_____
_____
_____
_____

2) Why do you want to become an actor? What moment in your life, event, movie, TV show, actor or memory you have, made you realize that becoming an actor was your calling, passion and something you must do?

_____
_____
_____
_____
_____
_____
_____
_____
_____
_____
_____
_____
_____
_____
_____
_____
_____
_____
_____
_____
_____
_____
_____

3) What are your deepest desires with acting? How far do you want to take acting? Do you want to be a mega movie star? A series regular? Book a huge national commercial?

*Go as big as you want to with this one! I want you to go beyond your wildest dreams and dream BIG!

Write your deepest desires with acting here:

_____
_____
_____
_____
_____
_____
_____
_____
_____
_____
_____
_____
_____
_____
_____
_____
_____
_____

4) WHAT IS YOUR GOAL(S)?

What is the most important goal(s) you need to achieve in order to start your journey on getting your foot in the door in TV & Film and becoming a consistently working actor right from where you are? It's okay to start off with just one goal and sometimes easier but if you can handle tackling more than one goal at a time feel free to do so.

For Example: Is it studying acting and learning a technique by getting into a drama program, conservatory or taking acting classes at a studio? Getting your headshots and resume done? Getting your reel done? Creating your website? Finding a monologue or a scene to audition with? Taking audition technique classes? Signing up for classes and meet and greets with Casting Director's, agents and managers? Networking with industry professionals? Auditioning more? Marketing yourself and brand more? Creating your own content? Getting you to a healthier place physically and or mentally?

Write your goal(s) here:

_____
_____
_____
_____
_____
_____
_____
_____
_____
_____

_____
_____
_____
_____
_____
_____
_____
_____
_____
_____
_____
_____
_____
_____
_____
_____
_____
_____
_____
_____
_____

Great Work! Now you know what your goal(s) is! It's time to get even clearer…

5) What are the necessary steps you need to take in order to achieve your goal(s)?

For Example: If "studying acting and learning a technique" is your goal then these may be the necessary steps you need to take in order to achieve it.

1. Revisit chapter 1 in this book for ideas and research those studios and schools mentioned at theactorahustle.com as well as others that could be an even better fit for you. Google until you find the top schools, programs or studios in your area that suit you and make a list of them and their contact information.

2. Contact or continue to research each school online and find out what their requirements are, what their teaching style is and if that style sounds like something you're interested in, how often classes are and if it fits your schedule, how much the classes or school is, when does it start or is it on-going and can you audit the class or attend a showcase to be sure you like the vibe.

3. Decide on a school, class or program that best suits you that you will register for.

4. Get your resources, finances and lifestyle in order to attend this school, class or program.

5. Register, audition, fill out application and pay for the school, class or program.

6. Start your first day of class.

*If there are any resources you need to contact, visit, subscribe to etc. List them as a step. For Example (If your goal is to go on more auditions, step one might be 1) create a profile on actorsaccess.com, mandy.com, imdbpro.com and oneononenyc.com)

Write your steps here for each goal:

Congrats! You've just started the hustle! You can't hustle without knowing what you want and what you need to do to go get it and now you're super clear on your goal and what you need to do in order to achieve it! Pat yourself on the back and let's keep moving forward.

*Remember every goal takes time and sometimes money to achieve.

6) How do you need to position yourself financially and time wise in order to achieve this goal(s) how does your lifestyle need to shift?

1. For Example: For every stage in your career that you're trying to reach you have to figure out how to position yourself in terms of time and finances. You need to be able to support yourself and or your goal so what has to change in your life to make sure your reach your goal? There's no room for excuses. I bartended nights, days, weekends took catering jobs, did real estate and sold business loans to make shit happen. I dealt with a lot and I'm sure there are others out there who have dealt with more like Taraji P. Henson who picked up and moved with her son to California with just a goal and a little bit of money in her pocket. But she gave her goals no excuse. She made it happen. I made it happen and I'm still making it happen so do what you have to do to make it HAPPEN! We all need a support system or need to be able to support ourselves in order to breathe and move through life freely and reach our goals. We all need to surround ourselves with healthy like-minded individuals in order to stay positive and reach our goals in a healthy way. We all need to make sure we take care of our mental and physical health so we can stay alive to see the day we reach our goals. And we all need to make the time to be able to achieve our goals. Your list might look more or less like this

2. Need new job (find ideal job type, hours & Pay)

3. Move back in with parents (have that conversation with them)

4. Get a roommate (put an ad out or ask around)

5. Find a babysitter (ask around or Google and find a reputable company)

6. Stop taking current classes because it's really not what I want to do

7. Save money (how much from each paycheck do I need to save to reach my goal?)

8. Change my circle of friends or just get really busy so it can fade out.

9. Move (start doing what truly makes you happy with healthier people or even alone and focus on yourself and goals)

10. Walk 1 mile every day

11. Jog for 15 minutes a day

12. Find a great therapist

13. Leave my boyfriend/ because they are unhealthy for me and not conducive to my growth as an actor.

14. Leave my girlfriend because they are unhealthy for me and not conducive to my growth as an actor.

15. Visualize my goals and dreams daily.

16. Meditate on my goals and dreams daily.

7) WHAT DO YOU NEED TO DO?

Write what you need to do to position yourself in order to start to take every step you listed to achieve your goal(s). Also write how you are going to fix this issue here:

_____
_____
_____
_____
_____
_____
_____
_____
_____
_____
_____
_____
_____
_____
_____
_____
_____
_____
_____
_____
_____
_____
_____
_____
_____

Now you are even more clear on what you need to do and shift in your life in order to hustle and make it happen. Great work on diving deep. I'm proud of you!

But we need to tackle something super important first just in case there is any resistance...

What is your biggest fear or excuse in trying to achieve this goal or even achieve the goal of getting your foot in the door and becoming a consistently working actor?

> *It's important to get clear on how you could be holding yourself back so you can give yourself the permission you need in order to move forward. We all have fears some have dozens, I know I did and still do. But we need to face the ones that are holding us back from living the life we deserve and were destined to live but first we need to shift the way we think.

For Example: When I decided I was going to look for an acting class to go to in NYC, I just knew I had the acting chops without even attending a single class. I could already see the teacher standing up and giving me a standing ovation and saying "bravo! Bravo! Shana! Why are you even studying? Go forth and start auditioning because you are already a star!" Until I attended Deena Levy's weekend workshop class (which helps you determine if you want to continue studying with her) and saw how much I didn't know and how amazing everyone was and all of a sudden I was afraid of looking weak and being one of those green actors who force the acting and takes years to learn how to hone their craft. My fear was that I wasn't good enough to be an actor and that I was going to be out shined and ultimately embarrassed and laughed at. I was used to slaying everything I did right from the beginning without much of a learning curve and here I was, faced with my first big huge challenge of not feeling like I was the best. I mean I didn't even feel like I was any good. But I had a goal and a dream since I was 8 or 9 years old and I couldn't let that negative stupid self-talk, talk me out of doing everything in my power to become the best. I knew I was blessed to even know what I was put here on this earth to accomplish so why allow what I don't know and have never experienced to hold me back? What if this is what I'm supposed to go through in order to become great? What if I bail on my goals and dreams of becoming an actor by giving myself the excuse of "this is too hard and bruising my ego too much and too different"? Where will I be then? I'll tell you where I wouldn't have been. I wouldn't have been on "Law & Order" cracking jokes with Iced T who is massively cool, or "Shades Of Blue" and had the best acting lessons from Ray Liotta or "Power" where I learned to break a script down like never before and understand the unwritten layers of a character and give more of what is asked of me for the sake of supporting and carrying out the writers story all while giving the audience what they want to see due to Larenz Tate's amazing teachings and conversations and Mario Van Peebles' awesome direction which taught me how TV really moves when being filmed and how to be more natural by movement or in an Oscar nominated film like "the Big Sick" and being able to improv so amazingly because of the writing and sharing the screen with one of the best improvisers and comedians in the game, Kumail Nanjiani. So don't let fear of the unknown stop you from getting what was gifted to you. It's already yours; you just have to decide that you are going to get it regardless of what your current state is because it is your divine right. Everything that could hold you back will start to move out of your way and a path to achieve your dreams and goals will start to form the second you decide to take action on those steps because that fear is all in your mind. You taking action will cause that fear to disappear one step at a time because you will begin to see the change in you and then momentum will override the fear and your mind will shift from fearing the goal(s) to believing they will absolutely happen. Be sure of that and take those steps knowing you will reach your goal no matter what. F.E.A.R. (False Evidence Appearing Real)

FACE YOUR FEARS

Here's a list of possible fears you may have.

1. I don't think I'm good enough.
2. I'm afraid to put myself out there and get embarrassed.
3. I'm afraid I'll fail.
4. I'm afraid of what my family and friends may think.
5. I don't think I have the look.
6. I'm not confident enough.
7. I can't afford it
8. I'm from (wherever you're from) Nobody makes it from here. What makes me any different?
9. I don't have what it takes.
10. It's too hard.
11. I'm afraid of a certain someone or people seeing me on TV because of what I've done in the past.
12. I don't know where to start.
13. I'm not that smart.

Now with that being said..

What are your fears?

Write what your biggest fear(s) or excuse(s) that is holding you back from achieving your goal(s) here:

*If you need help determining your goal(s), figuring out your action steps and what your fear is and suggestions on how to conger the fear and fill please feel free to book a one on one session with me. Visit theactorshustle.com

Whew!!!!!!!!! You are a boss! You got it all out. You know what you want, how to get what you want, how you could be holding yourself back from getting what you want and faced that fear and now you just have to decide if you're going to let the fear(s) win or are you going to let the best version of yourself and your dreams and goals win?

If you chose wisely as most hustlers do, then you chose to let the best version of yourself and your dreams and goals win.

I'm so proud of you!! And I appreciate you taking another positive step in life!!!!!

Now, I want you to take your goal(s), The action steps you listed to achieve your goal(s) and if you need to, add your list of things to do to position yourself in order to take the necessary steps to achieve your goal (getting your lifestyle, time, finances, circle, mental & physical health to where it need to be in order to achieve your goal) and put them all in one big clear and organized list.

For Example:

Goal:

Study acting and learn a technique that suits me in a drama program, conservatory or taking acting classes at a studio.

Steps:

1. Revisit chapter 1 in this book for ideas and research those studios and schools mentioned as well as others that could be

an even better fit you. Google until you find the top schools, programs or studios in your area that suit you and make a list of them and their contact information.

2. Contact or continue to research each school online and find out what their requirements are, what their teaching style is and if that style sounds like something you're interested in, how often classes are and if this its your schedule, how much the classes or school is, when does it start or is it on-going and can you audit the class or attend a showcase to be sure you like the vibe.

3. Decide on a school, class or program that best suits you that you will register for.

4. Get your resources, finances and lifestyle in order to attend this school, class or program.

5. Register, audition, fill out application and pay for the school, class or program.

6. Start your first day of class.

Lifestyle Change:

1. Need new job (ideal job type, hours & Pay).

2. Move back in with parents (have that conversation with them).

3. Get a roommate (put an ad out or ask around).

4. Find a babysitter (ask around or Google and find a reputable company).

5. Stop taking current classes because it's really not what I want to do.

6. Save money (how much from each paycheck do I need to save to reach my goal?)

7. Change my circle of friends or just get really busy so it can fade out.
8. Move (start doing what truly makes you happy with healthier people or even alone and focus on yourself and goals).
9. Walk 1 mile every day.
10. Jog for 15 minutes a day.
11. Find a great therapist.
12. Leave my boyfriend because they are unhealthy for me.
13. Leave my girlfriend because they are unhealthy for me.
14. Visualize my goals and dreams.
15. Meditate on my goals and dreams.

This list will help you visually see what needs to be done in a super clear way and help you enter the information into your calendar.

Write your list out here:

_____
_____
_____
_____
_____
_____
_____
_____
_____
_____

Now that your list is clear and organized I want you to put a date next to each action step you will take in order to make your goals happen. Then, fill out your personal Calendar by implementing your goal(s), each action step and lifestyle change on the chosen date into your calendar. So decide now when you are going to make those power moves and change your life.

You should be repeating some of your steps throughout your calendar because some goals take time and repetition. Also use the alarm feature on your phone and set alarms where your actual goal is written out and appears on your screen to alert you throughout the day so you are constantly reminded of what you must do in order to more forward and live your best life. Once that goal is complete remember to delete it from your alarm.

Now that you have completed your first goal(s) to get started on your Actors hustle take the time you need to accomplish them. But as soon as you do, come back to this portion of the book to set a new goal and get going on it. I want you to repeat exactly what you did in the workbook QnA for your initial goal(s) in order to determine your next moves and get super clear on how you are going to move forward in your career. Come back to this workbook QnA every time you need to set a new goal, get super clear and take massive action on them.

These next few questions will help guide you to knowing exactly what you want, getting super clear with your goals and the steps you need to take in order to achieve them.

1) WHAT DO I WANT TO ACHIEVE NEXT? WHAT IS THE MOST IMPORTANT GOAL(S) YOU NEED TO ACHIEVE IN ORDER TO CONTINUE YOUR JOURNEY ON GETTING YOUR FOOT IN THE DOOR IN TV & FILM AND BECOMING A CONSISTENTLY WORKING ACTOR RIGHT FROM WHERE YOU ARE?

For example: "I am" going to sign with a great agency.

Write all the things you are going to achieve next and inspired to do here:

I am

2) WHAT ARE YOUR DEEPEST DESIRES WITH ACTING? HOW FAR DO YOU WANT TO TAKE ACTING? DO YOU WANT TO BE A MEGA MOVIE STAR? A SERIES REGULAR? BOOK A HUGE NATIONAL COMMERCIAL?

*Go as big as you want to with this one! I want you to go beyond your wildest dreams and dream BIG! This exercise is for you to remind yourself of who you are and what you came to do just in case the goal(s) you just wrote out weren't big enough.

Write your deepest desires with acting here:

_____
_____
_____
_____
_____
_____
_____
_____
_____
_____
_____
_____
_____
_____

Great Work! Now you know what your goal(s) is! It's time to get even clearer...

3) What are the necessary action steps I need to take ASAP in order to achieve my new goal(s)?????

For Example: In order to sign with an agency, I need to research 10 agencies that would be a perfect fit for me and then see if they have any meet and greets or classes that I can sign up for.

> *If there are any resources you need to contact, visit, subscribe to etc. List them as a step. For Example (If your goal is to go on more auditions, step one might be 1) create a profile on actorsconnection.com and oneononenyc.com)

Write your steps here for each goal:

_____
_____
_____
_____
_____
_____
_____
_____
_____
_____
_____
_____
_____
_____

Congrats! You've just started the hustle! You can't hustle without knowing what you want and what you need to do to go get it and now you're super clear on your goal and what you need to do in order to achieve it! Pat yourself on the back and let's keep moving forward.

***Remember every goal takes time and sometimes money to achieve. But it is always possible.**

4) How do you need to position yourself financially and time wise in order to achieve this goal(s) how does your lifestyle need to shift?

1. For Example: For every stage in your career that you're trying to reach you have to figure out how to position yourself in terms of time and finances. You need to be able to support yourself and your goals so what has to change in your life to make sure your reach your goal? There's no room for excuses. I bartended nights, days, weekends took catering jobs, did real estate and sold business loans to make shit happen. I dealt with a lot and I'm sure there are others out there who have dealt with and are dealing more. We all need to surround ourselves with healthy like-minded individuals in order to stay positive and reach our goals in a healthy way. We all need to make sure we take care of our mental and physical health so we can stay alive to see the day we reach our goals. And we all need to make the time to be able to achieve our goals. So, your list might look more or less like this

2. Need new job (find ideal job type, hours & Pay)

3. Move back in with parents (have that conversation with them)

4. Get a roommate (put an ad out or ask around)

5. Find a babysitter (ask around or Google and find a reputable company)

6. Stop taking current classes because it's really not what I want to do

7. Save money (how much from each paycheck do I need to save to reach my goal?)

8. Change my circle of friends or just get really busy so it can fade out.

9. Move (start doing what truly makes you happy with healthier people or even alone and focus on yourself and goals)

10. Walk 1 mile every day

11. Jog for 15 minutes a day

12. Find a great therapist

13. Leave my boyfriend/ because they are unhealthy for me and not conducive to my growth as an actor.

14. Leave my girlfriend because they are unhealthy for me and not conducive to my growth as an actor.

15. Visualize my goals and dreams daily.

16. Meditate on my goals and dreams daily.

Write what you need to do to position yourself in order to start to take every step you listed to achieve your goal(s). Also write how you are going to fix this issue here:

_____
_____
_____
_____
_____
_____
_____
_____
_____
_____
_____

Now you are even more clear on what you need to do and shift in your life in order to hustle and make it happen. Great work on diving deep. I'm proud of you!

But we need to tackle something super important first just in case there is any resistance…

5) WHAT IS YOUR BIGGEST FEAR OR EXCUSE IN TRYING TO ACHIEVE THIS GOAL OR EVEN ACHIEVE THE GOAL OF GETTING YOUR FOOT IN THE DOOR AND BECOMING A CONSISTENTLY WORKING ACTOR?

*It's important to get clear on how you could be holding yourself back so you can give yourself the permission you need in order to move forward. We all have fears some have dozens, I know I did and still do. But we need to face the ones that are holding us back from living the life we deserve and were destined to live but first we need to shift the way we think.

For Example: I feared doing the work that I thought it would take to get a better agent. I feared facing these big time agents and asking them clear questions that would reveal to me if they would be a good fit and help me grow in my career. But why? Because I was a people pleaser and had difficulty speaking my truth and speaking up for myself. But when I took that leap of faith and faced my fears to meet with my current agency, asked them those key questions, and put my fears aside they were able to really see ME and how serious I was about my acting career and goals. It helped us build a great actor/agent relationship that has lasted for years. So facing whatever fear you have will hopefully help you override the fear and your mind will shift from fearing the goal(s) to believing they will absolutely happen. Be sure of that and take those steps knowing you will reach your goal no matter what.   F.E.A.R. (False Evidence Appearing Real)

FACE YOUR FEARS

Here's a list of possible fears you may have.

1. I don't think I'm good enough.
2. I'm afraid to put myself out there and get embarrassed.
3. I'm afraid I'll fail.
4. I'm afraid of what my family and friends may think.
5. I don't think I have the look.
6. I'm not confident enough.
7. I can't afford it.
8. I'm from (wherever you're from) Nobody makes it from here. What makes me any different?
9. I don't have what it takes.
10. It's too hard.
11. I'm afraid of a certain someone or people seeing me on TV because of what I've done in the past.
12. I don't know where to start.
13. I'm not that smart.

Now with that being said..

What are your fears?

Write what your biggest fear(s) or excuse(s) that is holding you back from achieving your goal(s) here:

_____
_____
_____
_____

*If you need help determining your goal(s), figuring out your action steps, what you fear and suggestions on how to conger the fear, please feel free to visit theactorshustle.com for other options and resources.

Whew!!!!!!!! You are a boss! You got it all out. You know what you want, how to get what you want, how you could be holding yourself back from getting what you want, faced that fear and now you just have to decide if you're going to let the fear(s) win or are you going to let the best version of yourself and your dreams and goals win?

If you chose wisely as most hustlers do, then you chose to let the best version of yourself and your dreams and goals win.

I'm so proud of you!! And I appreciate you taking another positive step in life towards choosing what's best for YOU and what makes you happy.

Now, I want you to take your goal(s), The action steps you listed to achieve your goal(s) and if you need to, add your list of things to do to position yourself in order to take the necessary steps to achieve your goal (getting your lifestyle, time, finances, immediate circle, mental & physical health to where it needs to be in order to achieve your goal(s)) and put them all in one big clear and organized list.

For Example:

Goal:

Sign with the perfect agency for me

Steps:

1. Revisit chapter 2 in this book where it mentions how to get an agent for ideas.

2. Sign up or audition for Oneonone or any other actor's resource that holds meet and greets and classes between agents and actors.

3. Research and make a list of 10 agencies along with their agents I think would be a perfect fit for me. And vice versa.

4. Sign up for the meet and greet or class with any of the agents on my list.

5. Choose a great scene or monologue to showcase my talent and product.

6. Follow up and set up initial meeting with agency.

7. Set up final meeting with agent and agency.

Lifestyle Change:

1. Need new job in order to pay for and have the time to take these meet & greets and classes (ideal job type, hours & Pay)

2. Move back in with parents to cut back on expenses (have that conversation with them)

3. Get a roommate to cut back on expenses (put an ad out or ask around)

4. Find a babysitter to be able to have the time to take classes and go to meet & greets. (Ask around or Google and find a reputable company)

5. Stop taking current classes because it's really not what I want to do

6. Save money to take these meet and greets and classes (how much from each paycheck do I need to save to reach my goal?)

7. Walk 1 mile every day for mental clarity and to raise my positive energy.

8. Visualize my goals and dreams because that will help me attract them even more.

9. Meditate on my goals and dreams.

This list will help you visually see what needs to be done in a super clear way and help you enter the information into your calendar.

Write your list out here:

_____
_____
_____
_____
_____
_____
_____
_____
_____
_____
_____
_____
_____
_____
_____
_____
_____

Now that your list is clear and organized I want you to put a date next to each action step you will take in order to make your goals happen. Then, fill out your personal Calendar by implementing your goal(s), each action step and lifestyle change on the chosen date into your calendar. So decide now when you are going to make those power moves and change your life.

You should be repeating some of your steps throughout your calendar because some goals take time and repetition. Also use the alarm feature on your phone and set alarms where your actual goal is written out and appears on your screen to alert you throughout the day so you are constantly reminded of what you must do in order to more forward and live your best life. Once that goal is complete remember to delete it from your alarm.

Now that you have completed your first goal(s) to get started on your Actors hustle take the time you need to accomplish them. But as soon as you do, come back to this portion of the book to set a new goal and get going on it. I want you to repeat exactly what you did in the workbook QnA for your initial goal(s) in order to determine your next moves and get super clear on how you are going to move forward in your career. Come back to this workbook QnA every time you need to set a new goal, get super clear and take massive action on them.

These next few questions will help guide you to knowing exactly what you want, getting super clear with your goals and the steps you need to take in order to achieve them.

1) What do I want to achieve next? What is the most important goal(s) you need to achieve in order to continue your journey on getting your foot in the door in TV & Film and becoming a consistently working actor right from where you are?

For example: "I am" going to sign with a great agency.

Write all the things you are going to achieve next and inspired to do here:

I am

_____
_____
_____
_____
_____
_____
_____
_____
_____
_____
_____
_____
_____
_____
_____
_____
_____

2) WHAT ARE YOUR DEEPEST DESIRES WITH ACTING? HOW FAR DO YOU WANT TO TAKE ACTING? DO YOU WANT TO BE A MEGA MOVIE STAR? A SERIES REGULAR? BOOK A HUGE NATIONAL COMMERCIAL?

*Go as big as you want to with this one! I want you to go beyond your wildest dreams and dream BIG! This exercise is for you to remind yourself of who you are and what you came to do just in case the goal(s) you just wrote out weren't big enough.

Write your deepest desires with acting here:

___
___
___
___
___
___
___
___
___
___
___
___
___

Great Work! Now you know what your goal(s) is! It's time to get even clearer…

3) WHAT ARE THE NECESSARY ACTION STEPS I NEED TO TAKE ASAP IN ORDER TO ACHIEVE MY NEW GOAL(S)?????

For Example: In order to sign with an agency, I need to research 10 agencies that would be a perfect fit for me and then see if they have any meet and greets or classes that I can sign up for.

*If there are any resources you need to contact, visit, subscribe to etc. List them as a step. For Example (If your goal is to go on more auditions, step one might be 1) create a profile on actorsconnection.com and onenonenyc.com)

Write your steps here for each goal:

_____
_____
_____
_____
_____
_____
_____
_____
_____
_____
_____
_____
_____
_____
_____

_____
_____
_____
_____
_____
_____
_____
_____
_____
_____
_____
_____
_____
_____
_____
_____
_____
_____
_____
_____

Congrats! You've just started the hustle! You can't hustle without knowing what you want and what you need to do to go get it and now you're super clear on your goal and what you need to do in order to achieve it! Pat yourself on the back and let's keep moving forward.

*Remember every goal takes time and sometimes money to achieve. But it is always possible.

4) How do you need to position yourself financially and time wise in order to achieve this goal(s) how does your lifestyle need to shift?

1. For Example: For every stage in your career that you're trying to reach you have to figure out how to position yourself in terms of time and finances. You need to be able to support yourself and your goals so what has to change in your life to make sure your reach your goal? There's no room for excuses. I bartended nights, days, weekends took catering jobs, did real estate and sold business loans to make shit happen. I dealt with a lot and I'm sure there are others out there who have dealt with and are dealing more. We all need to surround ourselves with healthy like-minded individuals in order to stay positive and reach our goals in a healthy way. We all need to make sure we take care of our mental and physical health so we can stay alive to see the day we reach our goals. And we all need to make the time to be able to achieve our goals. So, your list might look more or less like this

2. Need new job (find ideal job type, hours & Pay)

3. Move back in with parents (have that conversation with them)

4. Get a roommate (put an ad out or ask around)

5. Find a babysitter (ask around or Google and find a reputable company)

6. Stop taking current classes because it's really not what I want to do

7. Save money (how much from each paycheck do I need to save to reach my goal?)

8. Change my circle of friends or just get really busy so it can fade out.

9. Move (start doing what truly makes you happy with healthier people or even alone and focus on yourself and goals)

10. Walk 1 mile every day

11. Jog for 15 minutes a day

12. Find a great therapist

13. Leave my boyfriend/ because they are unhealthy for me and not conducive to my growth as an actor.

14. Leave my girlfriend because they are unhealthy for me and not conducive to my growth as an actor.

15. Visualize my goals and dreams daily.

16. Meditate on my goals and dreams daily.

Write what you need to do to position yourself in order to start to take every step you listed to achieve your goal(s). Also write how you are going to fix this issue here:

_____
_____
_____
_____
_____
_____
_____
_____
_____
_____
_____

_____
_____
_____
_____
_____
_____
_____
_____
_____
_____
_____
_____
_____
_____
_____
_____
_____
_____
_____
_____

Now you are even more clear on what you need to do and shift in your life in order to hustle and make it happen. Great work on diving deep. I'm proud of you!

But we need to tackle something super important first just in case there is any resistance…

5) WHAT IS YOUR BIGGEST FEAR OR EXCUSE IN TRYING TO ACHIEVE THIS GOAL OR EVEN ACHIEVE THE GOAL OF GETTING YOUR FOOT IN THE DOOR AND BECOMING A CONSISTENTLY WORKING ACTOR?

*It's important to get clear on how you could be holding yourself back so you can give yourself the permission you need in order to move forward. We all have fears some have dozens, I know I did and still do. But we need to face the ones that are holding us back from living the life we deserve and were destined to live but first we need to shift the way we think.

For Example: I feared doing the work that I thought it would take to get a better agent. I feared facing these big time agents and asking them clear questions that would reveal to me if they would be a good fit and help me grow in my career. But why? Because I was a people pleaser and had difficulty speaking my truth and speaking up for myself. But when I took that leap of faith and faced my fears to meet with my current agency, asked them those key questions, and put my fears aside they were able to really see ME and how serious I was about my acting career and goals. It helped us build a great actor/agent relationship that has lasted for years. So facing whatever fear you have will hopefully help you override the fear and your mind will shift from fearing the goal(s) to believing they will absolutely happen. Be sure of that and take those steps knowing you will reach your goal no matter what. F.E.A.R. (False Evidence Appearing Real)

FACE YOUR FEARS

Here's a list of possible fears you may have.

1. I don't think I'm good enough.
2. I'm afraid to put myself out there and get embarrassed.

3. I'm afraid I'll fail.
4. I'm afraid of what my family and friends may think.
5. I don't think I have the look.
6. I'm not confident enough.
7. I can't afford it.
8. I'm from (wherever you're from) Nobody makes it from here. What makes me any different?
9. I don't have what it takes.
10. It's too hard.
11. I'm afraid of a certain someone or people seeing me on TV because of what I've done in the past.
12. I don't know where to start.
13. I'm not that smart.

Now with that being said..

What are your fears?

Write what your biggest fear(s) or excuse(s) that is holding you back from achieving your goal(s) here:

_____
_____
_____
_____
_____
_____
_____

*If you need help determining your goal(s), figuring out your action steps, what you fear and suggestions on how to conger the fear, please feel free to visit theactorshustle.com for other options and resources.

Whew!!!!!!!! You are a boss! You got it all out. You know what you want, how to get what you want, how you could be holding yourself back from getting what you want, faced that fear and now you just have to decide if you're going to let the fear(s) win or are you going to let the best version of yourself and your dreams and goals win?

If you chose wisely as most hustlers do, then you chose to let the best version of yourself and your dreams and goals win.

I'm so proud of you!! And I appreciate you taking another positive step in life towards choosing what's best for YOU and what makes you happy.

Now, I want you to take your goal(s), The action steps you listed to achieve your goal(s) and if you need to, add your list of things to do to position yourself in order to take the necessary steps to achieve your goal (getting your lifestyle, time, finances, immediate circle, mental & physical health to where it needs to be in order to achieve your goal(s)) and put them all in one big clear and organized list.

For Example:

Goal:

Sign with the perfect agency for me

Steps:

1. Revisit chapter 2 in this book where it mentions how to get an agent for ideas.

2. Sign up or audition for Oneonone or any other actor's resource that holds meet and greets and classes between agents and actors.

3. Research and make a list of 10 agencies along with their agents I think would be a perfect fit for me. And vice versa.

4. Sign up for the meet and greet or class with any of the agents on my list.

5. Choose a great scene or monologue to showcase my talent and product.

6. Follow up and set up initial meeting with agency.

7. Set up final meeting with agent and agency.

Lifestyle Change:

1. Need new job in order to pay for and have the time to take these meet & greets and classes (ideal job type, hours & Pay)

2. Move back in with parents to cut back on expenses (have that conversation with them)

3. Get a roommate to cut back on expenses (put an ad out or ask around)

4. Find a babysitter to be able to have the time to take classes and go to meet & greets. (Ask around or Google and find a reputable company)

5. Stop taking current classes because it's really not what I want to do

6. Save money to take these meet and greets and classes (how much from each paycheck do I need to save to reach my goal?)

7. Walk 1 mile every day for mental clarity and to raise my positive energy.
8. Visualize my goals and dreams because that will help me attract them even more.
9. Meditate on my goals and dreams.

This list will help you visually see what needs to be done in a super clear way and help you enter the information into your calendar.

Write your list out here:

_____
_____
_____
_____
_____
_____
_____
_____
_____
_____
_____
_____
_____
_____
_____
_____
_____

Now that your list is clear and organized I want you to put a date next to each action step you will take in order to make your goals happen. Then, fill out your personal Calendar by implementing your goal(s), each action step and lifestyle change on the chosen date into your calendar. So decide now when you are going to make those power moves and change your life.

You should be repeating some of your steps throughout your calendar because some goals take time and repetition. Also use the alarm feature on your phone and set alarms where your actual goal is written out and appears on your screen to alert you throughout the day so you are constantly reminded of what you must do in order to more forward and live your best life. Once that goal is complete remember to delete it from your alarm.

Now that you have completed your first goal(s) to get started on your Actors hustle take the time you need to accomplish them. But as soon as you do, come back to this portion of the book to set a new goal and get going on it. I want you to repeat exactly what you did in the workbook QnA for your initial goal(s) in order to determine your next moves and get super clear on how you are going to move forward in your career. Come back to this workbook QnA every time you need to set a new goal, get super clear and take massive action on them.

These next few questions will help guide you to knowing exactly what you want, getting super clear with your goals and the steps you need to take in order to achieve them.

1) What do I want to achieve next? What is the most important goal(s) you need to achieve in order to continue your journey on getting your foot in the door in TV & Film and becoming a consistently working actor right from where you are?

For example: "I am" going to sign with a great agency.

Write all the things you are going to achieve next and inspired to do here:

I am

_____
_____
_____
_____
_____
_____
_____
_____
_____
_____
_____
_____
_____
_____
_____

2) What are your deepest desires with acting? How far do you want to take acting? Do you want to be a mega movie star? A series regular? Book a huge national commercial?

*Go as big as you want to with this one! I want you to go beyond your wildest dreams and dream BIG! This exercise is for you to remind yourself of who you are and what you came to do just in case the goal(s) you just wrote out weren't big enough.

Write your deepest desires with acting here:

_____
_____
_____
_____
_____
_____
_____
_____
_____
_____
_____
_____
_____
_____

Great Work! Now you know what your goal(s) is! It's time to get even clearer...

3) WHAT ARE THE NECESSARY ACTION STEPS I NEED TO TAKE ASAP IN ORDER TO ACHIEVE MY NEW GOAL(S)?????

For Example: In order to sign with an agency, I need to research 10 agencies that would be a perfect fit for me and then see if they have any meet and greets or classes that I can sign up for.

*If there are any resources you need to contact, visit, subscribe to etc. List them as a step. For Example (If your goal is to go on more auditions, step one might be 1) create a profile on actorsconnection.com and oneononenyc.com)

Write your steps here for each goal:

_____
_____
_____
_____
_____
_____
_____
_____
_____
_____
_____
_____
_____
_____
_____

_____
_____
_____
_____
_____
_____
_____
_____
_____
_____
_____
_____
_____
_____
_____
_____
_____
_____
_____
_____

Congrats! You've just started the hustle! You can't hustle without knowing what you want and what you need to do to go get it and now you're super clear on your goal and what you need to do in order to achieve it! Pat yourself on the back and let's keep moving forward.

*Remember every goal takes time and sometimes money to achieve. But it is always possible.

4) How do you need to position yourself financially and time wise in order to achieve this goal(s) how does your lifestyle need to shift?

1. For Example: For every stage in your career that you're trying to reach you have to figure out how to position yourself in terms of time and finances. You need to be able to support yourself and your goals so what has to change in your life to make sure your reach your goal? There's no room for excuses. I bartended nights, days, weekends took catering jobs, did real estate and sold business loans to make shit happen. I dealt with a lot and I'm sure there are others out there who have dealt with and are dealing more. We all need to surround ourselves with healthy like-minded individuals in order to stay positive and reach our goals in a healthy way. We all need to make sure we take care of our mental and physical health so we can stay alive to see the day we reach our goals. And we all need to make the time to be able to achieve our goals. So, your list might look more or less like this

2. Need new job (find ideal job type, hours & Pay)

3. Move back in with parents (have that conversation with them)

4. Get a roommate (put an ad out or ask around)

5. Find a babysitter (ask around or Google and find a reputable company)

6. Stop taking current classes because it's really not what I want to do

7. Save money (how much from each paycheck do I need to save to reach my goal?)

8. Change my circle of friends or just get really busy so it can fade out.

9. Move (start doing what truly makes you happy with healthier people or even alone and focus on yourself and goals)

10. Walk 1 mile every day

11. Jog for 15 minutes a day

12. Find a great therapist

13. Leave my boyfriend/ because they are unhealthy for me and not conducive to my growth as an actor.

14. Leave my girlfriend because they are unhealthy for me and not conducive to my growth as an actor.

15. Visualize my goals and dreams daily.

16. Meditate on my goals and dreams daily.

Write what you need to do to position yourself in order to start to take every step you listed to achieve your goal(s). Also write how you are going to fix this issue here:

_____
_____
_____
_____
_____
_____
_____
_____
_____
_____
_____

Now you are even more clear on what you need to do and shift in your life in order to hustle and make it happen. Great work on diving deep. I'm proud of you!

But we need to tackle something super important first just in case there is any resistance…

5) What is your biggest fear or excuse in trying to achieve this goal or even achieve the goal of getting your foot in the door and becoming a consistently working actor?

*It's important to get clear on how you could be holding yourself back so you can give yourself the permission you need in order to move forward. We all have fears some have dozens, I know I did and still do. But we need to face the ones that are holding us back from living the life we deserve and were destined to live but first we need to shift the way we think.

For Example: I feared doing the work that I thought it would take to get a better agent. I feared facing these big time agents and asking them clear questions that would reveal to me if they would be a good fit and help me grow in my career. But why? Because I was a people pleaser and had difficulty speaking my truth and speaking up for myself. But when I took that leap of faith and faced my fears to meet with my current agency, asked them those key questions, and put my fears aside they were able to really see ME and how serious I was about my acting career and goals. It helped us build a great actor/agent relationship that has lasted for years. So facing whatever fear you have will hopefully help you override the fear and your mind will shift from fearing the goal(s) to believing they will absolutely happen. Be sure of that and take those steps knowing you will reach your goal no matter what. F.E.A.R. (False Evidence Appearing Real)

FACE YOUR FEARS

Here's a list of possible fears you may have.

1. I don't think I'm good enough.

2. I'm afraid to put myself out there and get embarrassed.
3. I'm afraid I'll fail.
4. I'm afraid of what my family and friends may think.
5. I don't think I have the look.
6. I'm not confident enough.
7. I can't afford it.
8. I'm from (wherever you're from) Nobody makes it from here. What makes me any different?
9. I don't have what it takes.
10. It's too hard.
11. I'm afraid of a certain someone or people seeing me on TV because of what I've done in the past.
12. I don't know where to start.
13. I'm not that smart.

Now with that being said..

What are your fears?

Write what your biggest fear(s) or excuse(s) that is holding you back from achieving your goal(s) here:

_____
_____
_____
_____

> *If you need help determining your goal(s), figuring out your action steps, what you fear and suggestions on how to conger the fear, please feel free to visit theactorshustle.com for other options and resources.

Whew!!!!!!!! You are a boss! You got it all out. You know what you want, how to get what you want, how you could be holding yourself back from getting what you want, faced that fear and now you just have to decide if you're going to let the fear(s) win or are you going to let the best version of yourself and your dreams and goals win?

If you chose wisely as most hustlers do, then you chose to let the best version of yourself and your dreams and goals win.

I'm so proud of you!! And I appreciate you taking another positive step in life towards choosing what's best for YOU and what makes you happy.

Now, I want you to take your goal(s), The action steps you listed to achieve your goal(s) and if you need to, add your list of things to do to position yourself in order to take the necessary steps to achieve your goal (getting your lifestyle, time, finances, immediate circle, mental & physical health to where it needs to be in order to achieve your goal(s)) and put them all in one big clear and organized list.

For Example:

Goal:

Sign with the perfect agency for me

Steps:

1. Revisit chapter 2 in this book where it mentions how to get an agent for ideas.

2. Sign up or audition for Oneonone or any other actor's resource that holds meet and greets and classes between agents and actors.

3. Research and make a list of 10 agencies along with their agents I think would be a perfect fit for me. And vice versa.

4. Sign up for the meet and greet or class with any of the agents on my list.

5. Choose a great scene or monologue to showcase my talent and product.

6. Follow up and set up initial meeting with agency.

7. Set up final meeting with agent and agency.

Lifestyle Change:

1. Need new job in order to pay for and have the time to take these meet & greets and classes (ideal job type, hours & Pay)

2. Move back in with parents to cut back on expenses (have that conversation with them)

3. Get a roommate to cut back on expenses (put an ad out or ask around)

4. Find a babysitter to be able to have the time to take classes and go to meet & greets. (Ask around or Google and find a reputable company)

5. Stop taking current classes because it's really not what I want to do

6. Save money to take these meet and greets and classes (how much from each paycheck do I need to save to reach my goal?)

7. Walk 1 mile every day for mental clarity and to raise my positive energy.
8. Visualize my goals and dreams because that will help me attract them even more.
9. Meditate on my goals and dreams.

This list will help you visually see what needs to be done in a super clear way and help you enter the information into your calendar.

Write your list out here:

Now that your list is clear and organized I want you to put a date next to each action step you will take in order to make your goals happen. Then, fill out your personal Calendar by implementing your goal(s), each action step and lifestyle change on the chosen date into your calendar. So decide now when you are going to make those power moves and change your life.

You should be repeating some of your steps throughout your calendar because some goals take time and repetition. Also use the alarm feature on your phone and set alarms where your actual goal is written out and appears on your screen to alert you throughout the day so you are constantly reminded of what you must do in order to more forward and live your best life. Once that goal is complete remember to delete it from your alarm.

Now that you have completed your first goal(s) to get started on your Actors hustle take the time you need to accomplish them. But as soon as you do, come back to this portion of the book to set a new goal and get going on it. I want you to repeat exactly what you did in the workbook QnA for your initial goal(s) in order to determine your next moves and get super clear on how you are going to move forward in your career. Come back to this workbook QnA every time you need to set a new goal, get super clear and take massive action on them.

These next few questions will help guide you to knowing exactly what you want, getting super clear with your goals and the steps you need to take in order to achieve them.

1) WHAT DO I WANT TO ACHIEVE NEXT? WHAT IS THE MOST IMPORTANT GOAL(S) YOU NEED TO ACHIEVE IN ORDER TO CONTINUE YOUR JOURNEY ON GETTING YOUR FOOT IN THE DOOR IN TV & FILM AND BECOMING A CONSISTENTLY WORKING ACTOR RIGHT FROM WHERE YOU ARE?

For example: "I am" going to sign with a great agency.

Write all the things you are going to achieve next and inspired to do here:

I am

_____
_____
_____
_____
_____
_____
_____
_____
_____
_____
_____
_____
_____
_____
_____
_____
_____

2) What are your deepest desires with acting? How far do you want to take acting? Do you want to be a mega movie star? A series regular? Book a huge national commercial?

*Go as big as you want to with this one! I want you to go beyond your wildest dreams and dream BIG! This exercise is for you to remind yourself of who you are and what you came to do just in case the goal(s) you just wrote out weren't big enough.

Write your deepest desires with acting here:

_____
_____
_____
_____
_____
_____
_____
_____
_____
_____
_____
_____

Great Work! Now you know what your goal(s) is! It's time to get even clearer...

3) What are the necessary action steps I need to take ASAP in order to achieve my new goal(s)?????

For Example: In order to sign with an agency, I need to research 10 agencies that would be a perfect fit for me and then see if they have any meet and greets or classes that I can sign up for.

*If there are any resources you need to contact, visit, subscribe to etc. List them as a step. For Example (If your goal is to go on more auditions, step one might be 1) create a profile on actorsconnection.com and oneononenyc.com)

Write your steps here for each goal:

_____
_____
_____
_____
_____
_____
_____
_____
_____
_____
_____
_____
_____
_____
_____
_____
_____
_____
_____
_____

Congrats! You've just started the hustle! You can't hustle without knowing what you want and what you need to do to go get it and now you're super clear on your goal and what you need to do in order to achieve it! Pat yourself on the back and let's keep moving forward.

***Remember every goal takes time and sometimes money to achieve. But it is always possible.**

4) HOW DO YOU NEED TO POSITION YOURSELF FINANCIALLY AND TIME WISE IN ORDER TO ACHIEVE THIS GOAL(S) HOW DOES YOUR LIFESTYLE NEED TO SHIFT?

1. For Example: For every stage in your career that you're trying to reach you have to figure out how to position yourself in terms of time and finances. You need to be able to support yourself and your goals so what has to change in your life to make sure your reach your goal? There's no room for excuses. I bartended nights, days, weekends took catering jobs, did real estate and sold business loans to make shit happen. I dealt with a lot and I'm sure there are others out there who have dealt with and are dealing more. We all need to surround ourselves with healthy like-minded individuals in order to stay positive and reach our goals in a healthy way. We all need to make sure we take care of our mental and physical health so we can stay alive to see the day we reach our goals. And we all need to make the time to be able to achieve our goals. So, your list might look more or less like this

2. Need new job (find ideal job type, hours & Pay)

3. Move back in with parents (have that conversation with them)

4. Get a roommate (put an ad out or ask around)

5. Find a babysitter (ask around or Google and find a reputable company)

6. Stop taking current classes because it's really not what I want to do

7. Save money (how much from each paycheck do I need to save to reach my goal?)

8. Change my circle of friends or just get really busy so it can fade out.

9. Move (start doing what truly makes you happy with healthier people or even alone and focus on yourself and goals)

10. Walk 1 mile every day

11. Jog for 15 minutes a day

12. Find a great therapist

13. Leave my boyfriend/ because they are unhealthy for me and not conducive to my growth as an actor.

14. Leave my girlfriend because they are unhealthy for me and not conducive to my growth as an actor.

15. Visualize my goals and dreams daily.

16. Meditate on my goals and dreams daily.

Write what you need to do to position yourself in order to start to take every step you listed to achieve your goal(s). Also write how you are going to fix this issue here:

_____
_____
_____
_____
_____
_____
_____
_____
_____
_____

_____
_____
_____
_____
_____
_____
_____
_____
_____
_____
_____
_____
_____
_____
_____
_____
_____
_____
_____
_____
_____
_____
_____

Now you are even more clear on what you need to do and shift in your life in order to hustle and make it happen. Great work on diving deep. I'm proud of you!

But we need to tackle something super important first just in case there is any resistance…

5) WHAT IS YOUR BIGGEST FEAR OR EXCUSE IN TRYING TO ACHIEVE THIS GOAL OR EVEN ACHIEVE THE GOAL OF GETTING YOUR FOOT IN THE DOOR AND BECOMING A CONSISTENTLY WORKING ACTOR?

*It's important to get clear on how you could be holding yourself back so you can give yourself the permission you need in order to move forward. We all have fears some have dozens, I know I did and still do. But we need to face the ones that are holding us back from living the life we deserve and were destined to live but first we need to shift the way we think.

For Example: I feared doing the work that I thought it would take to get a better agent. I feared facing these big time agents and asking them clear questions that would reveal to me if they would be a good fit and help me grow in my career. But why? Because I was a people pleaser and had difficulty speaking my truth and speaking up for myself. But when I took that leap of faith and faced my fears to meet with my current agency, asked them those key questions, and put my fears aside they were able to really see ME and how serious I was about my acting career and goals. It helped us build a great actor/agent relationship that has lasted for years. So facing whatever fear you have will hopefully help you override the fear and your mind will shift from fearing the goal(s) to believing they will absolutely happen. Be sure of that and take those steps knowing you will reach your goal no matter what.   F.E.A.R. (False Evidence Appearing Real)

FACE YOUR FEARS

Here's a list of possible fears you may have.

1. I don't think I'm good enough.

2. I'm afraid to put myself out there and get embarrassed.
3. I'm afraid I'll fail.
4. I'm afraid of what my family and friends may think.
5. I don't think I have the look.
6. I'm not confident enough.
7. I can't afford it.
8. I'm from (wherever you're from) Nobody makes it from here. What makes me any different?
9. I don't have what it takes.
10. It's too hard.
11. I'm afraid of a certain someone or people seeing me on TV because of what I've done in the past.
12. I don't know where to start.
13. I'm not that smart.

Now with that being said..

What are your fears?

Write what your biggest fear(s) or excuse(s) that is holding you back from achieving your goal(s) here:

_____
_____
_____
_____
_____

*If you need help determining your goal(s), figuring out your action steps, what you fear and suggestions on how to conger the fear, please feel free to visit theactorshustle.com for other options and resources.

Whew!!!!!!!! You are a boss! You got it all out. You know what you want, how to get what you want, how you could be holding yourself back from getting what you want, faced that fear and now you just have to decide if you're going to let the fear(s) win or are you going to let the best version of yourself and your dreams and goals win?

If you chose wisely as most hustlers do, then you chose to let the best version of yourself and your dreams and goals win.

I'm so proud of you!! And I appreciate you taking another positive step in life towards choosing what's best for YOU and what makes you happy.

Now, I want you to take your goal(s), The action steps you listed to achieve your goal(s) and if you need to, add your list of things to do to position yourself in order to take the necessary steps to achieve your goal (getting your lifestyle, time, finances, immediate circle, mental & physical health to where it needs to be in order to achieve your goal(s)) and put them all in one big clear and organized list.

For Example:

Goal:

Sign with the perfect agency for me

Steps:

1. Revisit chapter 2 in this book where it mentions how to get an agent for ideas.

2. Sign up or audition for Oneonone or any other actor's resource that holds meet and greets and classes between agents and actors.

3. Research and make a list of 10 agencies along with their agents I think would be a perfect fit for me. And vice versa.

4. Sign up for the meet and greet or class with any of the agents on my list.

5. Choose a great scene or monologue to showcase my talent and product.

6. Follow up and set up initial meeting with agency.

7. Set up final meeting with agent and agency.

Lifestyle Change:

1. Need new job in order to pay for and have the time to take these meet & greets and classes (ideal job type, hours & Pay)

2. Move back in with parents to cut back on expenses (have that conversation with them)

3. Get a roommate to cut back on expenses (put an ad out or ask around)

4. Find a babysitter to be able to have the time to take classes and go to meet & greets. (Ask around or Google and find a reputable company)

5. Stop taking current classes because it's really not what I want to do

6. Save money to take these meet and greets and classes (how much from each paycheck do I need to save to reach my goal?)

7. Walk 1 mile every day for mental clarity and to raise my positive energy.

8. Visualize my goals and dreams because that will help me attract them even more.

9. Meditate on my goals and dreams.

This list will help you visually see what needs to be done in a super clear way and help you enter the information into your calendar.

Write your list out here:

_____
_____
_____
_____
_____
_____
_____
_____
_____
_____
_____
_____
_____
_____
_____
_____
_____

Now that your list is clear and organized I want you to put a date next to each action step you will take in order to make your goals happen. Then, fill out your personal Calendar by implementing your goal(s), each action step and lifestyle change on the chosen date into your calendar. So decide now when you are going to make those power moves and change your life.

You should be repeating some of your steps throughout your calendar because some goals take time and repetition. Also use the alarm feature on your phone and set alarms where your actual goal is written out and appears on your screen to alert you throughout the day so you are constantly reminded of what you must do in order to more forward and live your best life. Once that goal is complete remember to delete it from your alarm.

Now that you have completed your first goal(s) to get started on your Actors hustle take the time you need to accomplish them. But as soon as you do, come back to this portion of the book to set a new goal and get going on it. I want you to repeat exactly what you did in the workbook QnA for your initial goal(s) in order to determine your next moves and get super clear on how you are going to move forward in your career. Come back to this workbook QnA every time you need to set a new goal, get super clear and take massive action on them.

www.ingramcontent.com/pod-product-compliance
Lightning Source LLC
Chambersburg PA
CBHW050313120526
44592CB00014B/1894